DIVINE
RELATIONSHIPS
Two Bodies, One Soul

NAM KAUR KHALSA
& SIRI ATMA SINGH KHALSA, M.D.

BASED ON THE TEACHINGS OF YOGI BHAJAN™

Credits

Production Manager: Nam Kaur Khalsa

Photographer: Alberto Bevacqua

Female Model: Anna Petrova (Ammandeep)

Male Model: Dru Lockwood

Book Design, Layout & Cover: Guru Raj Kaur Khalsa

Editorial Consultant: Siri Neel Kaur Khalsa, KRI

Consulting Editor: Arnbjörg Kristín Konráðsdóttir

Publisher: Yogic Reality Inc.

YOGIC REALITY
pure healing

ISBN 978-0-615-28385-2

Love Lessons

Dedicated to my beloved Teacher, Yogi Bhajan

"Love is standing under the other person," you said.
You have done so time and again.

"I'll take away all your tears, but you must drop your fears," was your promise.
And you delivered.

"Never show your weakness to another, give it to God," was your advice.
A gem of wisdom I treasure.

"Whether someone compliments or complains, hear only God needing to talk."
Thank you for taking my ego out of it.

"The essence of your soul is the vibration of the Word of God."
I have realized that nourishment comes from the Naam.

"Become me with a thin skin," was the answer you gave.
It keeps you with me always.

"Live in love of God and all that is shall be yours."
In gratitude I live by your hallmarks of love.

All love in divine, Nam Kaur

Foreword

I've had the pleasure of knowing Nam Kaur and Dr. Siri Atma for many years now, and one of the most amazing things about them is that they are the most beautiful couple imaginable. And that is what Divine Relationships is – a how-to manual – how to have a true, deep, loving relationship with your significant other.

As teachers, they cut right to the chase, and that is why I have such respect for them both. They always focus on the most important aspects of every single circumstance, while having fun, loving life and each other, and serving with nobility and grace.

Divine Relationships reads like a warm fireside chat, answering the hard questions, covering material no one else has, in a cozy, easy-to-read format. I hope you enjoy it and find it as useful and informative as I have.

Akal Sahai Singh
www.bethelighthouse.com

Introduction

Under a striped yellow and white canopy at Women's Camp, I sit amid a hundred young women, entertained and inspired by engaging stories, timeless wisdom from the East, Q & A sessions, and meditating with the Master of Kundalini Yoga. Some evenings Yogi Bhajan is humorous and light, driving right up to the tent in his Willys Jeep. Tonight his words impart his heartfelt belief that women can change the world, and a summer rainstorm pelts the tent for emphasis. Little did I know then, that thirty years later I would study these lectures to present the essence of his teachings for couples.

For me, the most fascinating part of the research for *Divine Relationships* was discovering new benefits for classics that Yogi Bhajan taught from the start, like *Kirtan Kriya* and *Grace of God*. I considered myself well-versed in his teachings before I began, but was quite surprised to find, for example, that the Yogi Tea recipe comes from an ancient scripture on sex for women! I hope you'll delight in what you discover.

Nam Kaur Khalsa

A relationship is an exchange between two or more objects. A divine relationship then is a divine exchange between two people. Most of the work of a divine relationship is in the unspoken world where I live to my highest self, and I hold my grace and space. It is formed out of my thoughts, and more importantly, my intention. There can be no merger without purity of intention.

Purity of intention involves service, authenticity, and the joy of belonging or merging into something greater than the individual self. Authenticity means that you are what you are. A peach tree bears peaches, not apples. Service doesn't mean running around doing things for others, it mean allowing others to take what they need from you. Service stands at the base of a divine relationship. Your fulfillment comes from enjoying the purity of your own intent, and the peace that occurs when someone finds their completion in your presence. As you serve in this way, you become one with yourself and your partner. You merge into a divine grace.

Sat Nam, Siri Atma Singh

Contents

1

Two Bodies, One Soul

You must connect with your soul
in this lifetime to achieve anything divine.

What is a divine relationship? One in which both partners desire to achieve a sense of oneness. In a divine relationship the goal is to merge and become two bodies and one soul. Merger is the alignment of two electromagnetic fields so the consciousness, the truth they live, is in harmony. This may sound mysterious, but the soul is a nugget of truth, so becoming one soul means sharing and living one truth.

> *He never knows the "she" and she never knows the*
> *"he" until they both merge in higher consciousness.*
> — YOGI BHAJAN

People fear that if they invest in a relationship and become something new, the other person may walk away with a piece of them. They wonder if they will lose their individual identity. The beauty of merger is that you retain your uniqueness and merge with your partner.

> *Love is a consciousness of living in*
> *another being and experiencing yourself.*
> — YOGI BHAJAN

Using the tools of Kundalini Yoga as taught by Yogi Bhajan™, you can create a more loving and committed relationship in which you and your partner merge. If you don't have a partner, many of these tools can help you attract a spiritual mate.

We'll use what yogis believe to be the secret of life – the power of the word. Changing the vibration of your day-to-day communication with your partner will have immediate impact, while the use of mantras in meditation will have subtle, long-term effects.

The Ten Bodies

The concept of having ten bodies is unique to Kundalini Yoga and is inter-woven throughout *Divine Relationships*. Your "self" is made up of five bodies: the soul, the negative, positive, and neutral minds, and the physical body. The phrase "body, mind, and soul" actually refers to these five bodies. The more elusive bodies are the arcline, the aura, the pranic body, the subtle body, and the radiant body.

FIRST BODY
THE SOUL BODY

The soul is the timeless body which contains your being – your conscious-ness and personality. The sensitivity of your soul tells you what is right and wrong for you. It is this sensitivity which is the source of your happiness. You must connect with your soul in this lifetime to achieve anything divine.

> *The dance of the spirit is called soul....It is the flow of the spirit of Infinity into the finite. The soul is the finite aspect of Infinity; it is a part of Infinity.*
> –YOGI BHAJAN

THE MIND

The mind – your mental body – is very strong because it is a triple body. Ideally the mind serves as a mental calculator to consciously guide you. When your mind is under the guidance of your soul, you can balance the waves of thoughts and feelings that continuously arise. But if you allow your mind to control you, it will calculate how to avoid what it fears, how to get what it wants, and how to get even with whatever gets in its way.

SECOND BODY
THE NEGATIVE MIND
The job of your negative mind is to calculate risk and protect you. It automatically negates everything that comes your way no matter how positive it may be. It surveys the situation and tells you all the negatives. If you misunderstand the role of your negative mind, the barrage of negative thoughts can fill you with fear and doubt.

THIRD BODY
THE POSITIVE MIND
The job of your positive mind is to make you aware of all the benefits in a situation. But be careful as the positive mind can also unload information from your subconscious memory to support the thoughts of the negative mind, preventing you from making a clear decision.

FOURTH BODY
THE NEUTRAL MIND
Without a balanced neutral mind you cannot be constant and carefree and discover who you are. The neutral mind evaluates the risks and benefits that the negative and positive minds calculate, so you can understand what is best for you. The principle of the neutral mind is to be dutiful; it guides you to create win-win solutions.

FIFTH BODY
THE PHYSICAL BODY
The physical body is a vehicle to coordinate all your activity on the physical plane so you can be successful doing what you have to do in life. If you relate only to your physical body you will become depressed when it fails. To be happy, train your physical body to call on the other nine bodies.

SIXTH BODY
THE ARCLINE

The arcline is your body of magnetic purity. Like a halo, it stretches from earlobe to earlobe. When your arcline is strong it protects you from the thoughts and projections of people who are far away. Your arcline can be reflective or dull – it is a measurement of your overall energy. Calmness is seen in your arcline. When you emit light which touches the tips of other people's arclines and auras, this is called "grace."

SEVENTH BODY
THE AURA

The aura is your body of magnetic sensitivity. All the pain and pleasure you experience is recorded in your aura. Your intuitive sense lies within your auric body and gives you sensitivity to circumstances and people in your immediate environment. The human body can have an aura of up to nine feet. A dense aura makes you act inappropriately while an expansive aura enhances your angelic nature and your health.

EIGHTH BODY
THE PRANIC BODY

The pranic body is the electromagnetic body of life and the source of your sense of humor. A yogi is aware of the pranic body when practicing breath control. When your breath is not deep enough to meet the needs of the physical body, then your relationships, your behavior and your life will all be unbalanced. There is a strong relationship between the pranic and physical bodies. Yogis have used this relationship for thousands of years to cure illness and lengthen life.

If you do not breathe consciously for 11 minutes a day,
you lose 40 percent of the vitality of life. This 40 percent
you cannot recapture by any medicine or any exercise.

– YOGI BHAJAN

NINTH BODY
THE SUBTLE BODY
Within the subtle body is awareness of the soul, i.e., self-awareness. Common sense arises from the subtle body. It enables you to understand the subtleties of life and learn quickly. Thoughts from the subtle body refine input from the soul. The soul may say: *Taking this action would be good.* The subtle body makes distinctions: *This is good; this would be better; and that would be best of all.* The subtle body is strengthened by meditation, noble acts and refined speech.

TENTH BODY
THE RADIANT BODY
The radiant body is the electromagnetic projection of the essence of the other nine bodies. Your radiance depends on the amount of *prana* (life force) you consume. The radiant body's magnetic attraction gives you courage. When it is strong, you are bright, influential and prosperous; when clouded by fear, it cannot work. When your radiant body is strong, success is automatic.

Tuning-In to Begin
Ong Namo Guru Dev Namo

Before you begin any of the yoga or meditation given in *Divine Relation-ships*, be sure to tune-in. Sit in Easy Pose with your spine straight. Press your hands together in Prayer Pose at the center of the chest, sides of the thumbs pressed against the sternum. With your eyes closed, focus your concentration at the Third Eye Point located between the eyebrows at the root of the nose, about a half inch under the skin.

Inhale deeply and as you exhale chant the Adi Mantra, *Ong Namo Guru Dev Namo*, on one breath. The sound *Dev* is chanted a minor third higher than the other sounds. If you cannot chant it all on one breath, take a short breath after *Ong Namo*. Repeat the mantra three times. You can hear the Adi Mantra chanted online at www.kriteachings.org in the Tools for Students & Teachers section under Kundalini Yoga Mantras.

Ong   Na-mo   Gu- roo Dev   Na- mo

The meaning of *Ong Namo Guru Dev Namo* is: *I call on the creative infinite consciousness of the universe. I call on the divine wisdom within me.*

If you are new to Kundalini Yoga, there is an informative chapter on the basics and terminology you will need to know to get started – see Chapter 10, Kundalini Yoga Basics, page 148.

Ong Namo Guru Dev Namo

2
Attracting a Spiritual Partner

Your attraction, your confidence, your sensory system, and your psyche, will all work to attract a spiritual partner for you.

You all try to find your soul mate without finding your own soul.
The problem is that we want to emotionally attach to somebody.
How can your attachment ever be true if you have never attached
yourself to your soul, to your consciousness.

– Yogi Bhajan

We all search for someone special to be in relationship with. We long for the experience of being in love. Movies and music fill our hearts with unrealistic expectations, setting us up for failure long before our first kiss. Our idea of love is based on fantasy, and our desire for intimacy often leads us to pick partners who are less than ideal for us.

The problem you face is inside you. You seek affirmation of who you are from a mate. You want someone to complete you and make you divine. Eager to be loved, you may pretend to be what you are not to impress the opposite sex. Instead, establish a relationship with your own soul and discover who you were created to be.

If you live your life with a sense of adventure – as if you would never find a partner – you are more likely to meet someone along the way. Don't change yourself just to meet someone; the relationship will only be temporary.

Each time you are romantically hurt it leaves a scar in your aura. Your hopeful innocence is lost. Carrying the painful memories into a new relationship makes you fearful and insecure. This is true for both sexes. Painful break-ups make it hard to move on, because in an effort to protect you, your negative mind reminds the positive mind of your past.

If you want to avoid this emotional roller coaster, consciously seek a partner who has more strength and commitment than charisma, someone capable of deep honesty and soulfulness.

When we teach relationship workshops, the question invariably arises, "How can I find a spiritual partner, someone with integrity?" First you must know how to recognize caliber and spirituality in the opposite sex. To do so you must drop your flirtatious behavior.

Flirting creates holes in a woman's aura and prevents her from being a good judge of character. When she flirts, a woman sacrifices her grace for flattery and attention. When a man flirts, he is generally after one thing and women know it – a casual fling without commitment.

> *Love is blind only when you are sensually involved.*
> *Love is very flowery and rosy when you are*
> *emotionally involved. Love is very dreamy when*
> *you are mentally involved. And love is very light,*
> *pure and conscious when your soul is involved.*
> —Yogi Bhajan

Flirting arouses sexual feelings and invites amorous involvement. If you have a flirtatious nature it's not easy to find a committed partner as like attracts like. A woman who is sophisticated and solid will attract a man of caliber. A man looking for a spiritual partner will seek a radiant and graceful woman.

When a woman flirts to attract the opposite sex, she drops her guard and men can take advantage of her. To overcome this tendency and become self-contained, a woman can practice *Kirtan Kriya* and the *Grace of God* meditation. Men can learn to relate to women gracefully by practicing the male version of the *Grace of God* meditation.

At every moment you have the chance to make conscious choices. Before you act, ask yourself, "Will this add to my grace?" Listen for the voice of your soul, it will answer you. If you live consciously, you will be content and self-contained. Once you are you and you are content, your attraction, your confidence, your sensory system, and your psyche will all work to attract a spiritual partner for you.

> *If you have caliber, and you have a commitment,*
> *then you can define very well what relationship*
> *you want.*
> —Yogi Bhajan

Cosmic Injury
by Yogi Bhajan

IN AMERICA YOU ARE TOLD, "go and find your mate." You date and end up with pits, and then you get married and divorced. Once you are emotionally hurt it creates a scar in your aura, a pain or "cosmic injury" in the subconscious, your positive mind. The negative mind forces the positive mind to remind you of that injury.

You can have every wealth in the world but you will be deprived of happiness and strength because of these cosmic injuries. They cause people to betray and lie.

Find a man who through time and space shall be your mate, who has strength, not charm. And find a female mate who has strength, not charm. Don't sell cheap for charm.

Your mental body will revert back to these memories, and you will react and react and react. The only reason to remember your past is to be grateful that you are not in it.

Edited excerpts from a lecture by Yogi Bhajan (December 1985)

Kriya to Release the Pain of the Past & Energize Your Current Relationship

(originally called Essence of Self)

When you are weighed down by the scars and disappointment in love, it is difficult to sense a brighter future. The pain blocks the inflow of cosmic energy and you become less sensitive to the possibilities life offers.

This kriya guides *prana* (life force) to the heart chakra, opening your heart so you can give and receive love without fear, anger or resentment. In this state of compassion you release the pain of your past relationships, energize your current relationship to a higher level, and begin to express your divine essence.

ONE

Sit in Easy Pose, arms extended to the front parallel to the floor with the palms facing down. Spread the arms slightly to form a V and rotate them backward in large circles as pictured. Begin Breath of Fire and gradually increase the power of the breath as you rotate the arms faster and faster, wider and wider. Continue energetically for **4 minutes**.

TWO

Lie on your stomach in Bow Pose. Rock
back and forth from the shoulders to the
knees coordinating the motion with a
powerful Breath of Fire, so
powerful that it feels as though fire is
coming from the nostrils. **1 minute**

THREE

Lie on your back and
clasp your knees to your
chest. Lift your forehead
to your knees and rock
along the entire length of
the spine in coordination
with Breath of Fire for
1½ minutes.

FOUR

Squat in Crow Pose with your hands clasped in Venus Lock
(see below) on top of your head. Inhale and rise up to a standing
position, exhale and squat down into Crow Pose **26 times**.

Venus Lock for MEN: With the palms facing each other, interlace the fingers with the left little
finger on the bottom. Put the left thumb tip just above the base of the right thumb on the
webbing between the thumb and index finger of the right hand. The right thumb tip presses
the fleshy mound at the base of the left thumb. Venus Lock for WOMEN: Women reverse the
sequence of alternating the fingers so that the right little finger is on the bottom and the tip of
the left thumb presses the fleshy mound of the right thumb.

FIVE Repeat exercise one for **2 minutes**.
On the physical level these exercises release tension, strengthen the digestion, and open the lungs.

SIX

Sit in Easy Pose and cross your hands over your chest at the Heart Center. Close your eyes. As you meditate, drop any self-limitations and experience your essence. You may also sing *Dhan Dhan Ram Das Guru* (Sangeet Kaur's version recommended), beaming from your Heart Center. Call out to Guru Ram Das to open your heart and create a miracle in your life. **11-31 minutes**

Kirtan Kriya

(also known as Sa-Ta-Na-Ma Meditation)

Kirtan Kriya brings emotional balance and healing to your psyche. The ring and index fingers are electrically negative relative to your other fingers. Vibrating on each fingertip alternates the electrical polarities, creating balance in the electromagnetic projection of your aura.

As you press the fingers and thumbs and vibrate *Sa Ta Na Ma*, your ego – represented by the thumbs – seals the effect of each mudra in your consciousness:

  Index finger: Gyan Mudra, knowledge.
  Middle finger: Shuni Mudra, wisdom, patience and intelligence.
  Ring finger: Surya Mudra, vitality.
  Little finger: Buddhi Mudra, the ability to communicate.

Posture & Eye Focus: Keep your spine straight and apply Chin Lock. Meditate at the Brow Point. As you chant, visualize the sound following the Golden Cord (the pathway between the pineal and pituitary glands), in an L shape, starting at the Crown Chakra at the top of your head, and projecting out your Third Eye to Infinity.

Mantra: *Sa Ta Na Ma* (pronounced *Saa Taa Naa Maa*), represents the Cycle of Creation. *Sa* means Infinity, cosmos, beginning; *Ta* means life, existence; *Na* is death, change, transformation; and *Ma* is rebirth. One repetition of the mantra takes 3-4 seconds. You can hear it (under *Kirtan Kriya* or *Panj Shabd*) chanted online at www.kriteachings.org in the Tools for Students & Teachers section under Kundalini Yoga Mantras.

Mudra: Start with the hands on your knees, elbows straight. As you chant, firmly press the tips of the fingers of each hand in turn to your thumb tips. On *Sa* the index/Jupiter fingers; on *Ta* the middle/Saturn fingers; on *Na* the ring/Sun fingers; and on *Ma* the pinky/Mercury fingers.

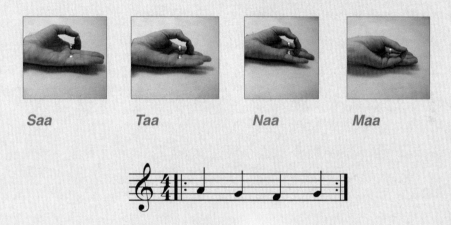

Saa   Taa   Naa   Maa

Chanting: *Kirtan Kriya* is chanted in the three languages of consciousness in the following pattern: for **5 minutes** chant in a normal voice, the language of humans; then in a strong whisper for **5 minutes**, in the language of lovers; for **10 minutes** vibrate the mantra silently, in the language of the divine; whisper for **5 minutes**; and then return to your normal voice for **5 minutes**. Inhale and suspend the breath as long as comfortable and then exhale. Sit in silence for the last minute of this **31 minute meditation**.

To End: Inhale, exhale, and stretch the spine, raising your hands up as far as possible, fingers spread wide. Take several deep breaths and then relax.

Timing: The duration of *Kirtan Kriya* may vary as long as the proportion of the three languages remains consistent, as in **5-5-10-5-5** or **2-2-4-2-2**, with a minute of silence at the end.

Grace of God Meditation

If a woman practices *Grace of God* for a year her aura will become tipped with gold or silver. This meditation balances the five elements and evokes a woman's grace, strength, and radiance. The power of the affirmation affects your thoughts, behavior, and personality and develops physical health, patience, and healing ability. It enables women to channel their emotions positively, drop their weaknesses, and develop effective communication. During menopause it is recommended that women do the *Grace of God* meditation five times a day.

Timing: Practice on an empty stomach twice a day for 40 days.

Mantra:

For women: *I am Grace of God*

For men: *I am in the Grace of God*.

PART ONE

Relax on your back with your eyes closed. Inhale deeply, hold the breath in, and silently repeat the mantra **ten times**; exhale completely, hold the breath out and silently repeat the mantra **ten times**. Repeat **five times** for a total of **100 repetitions**.

PART TWO

Relax your breath and with your eyes still closed, slowly come into Easy Pose. Put your right hand on your knee in Gyan Mudra, with the tips of the thumb and index finger pressed together. Raise your left hand as if taking an oath, palm facing forward. Repeat the mantra aloud **five times** as you tense each finger, one at a time, meditating on its governing energy. Keep the other fingers straight and relaxed. Start with the pinky finger and end with the thumb, for a total of **25 repetitions**. Relax the raised hand and meditate silently for a few minutes.

FINGER	GOVERNING PLANET	MUDRA	ELEMENT	ASPECTS INFLUENCED
Index finger	Jupiter	Gyan	Ether	Wisdom & expansion, ability to change
Middle finger	Saturn	Shuni	Air	Channel emotion to devotion and patience
Ring finger	Sun & Venus	Surya	Fire	Physical health, vitality, grace, and beauty
Pinky finger	Mercury	Buddhi	Water	Power to relate; subconscious communication with self
Thumb	None		Earth	Positive ego

3

The Difference Between the Sexes

A man's potency depends on the mental frequency and strength of a woman's aura.

What is the biggest difference between men and women? A woman's aura contains sixteen times more antennae per square millimeter than a man's, and her radiant body is sixteen times stronger. This gives women heightened electromagnetic power and makes all their faculties sixteen times stronger.

> *Every woman has sixteen times more talent than a man,*
> *intuition than a man, and intelligence than a man.*
> *This is a gift to her because she is made to process motherhood.*
>
> —Yogi Bhajan

All of a woman's qualities – both negative and positive – carry sixteen times the impact of a man's. When women hear they are sixteen times more powerful than men they are flattered. But a woman can also be sixteen times more destructive to herself and her partner, so she needs to have sixteen times the discipline.

Men may question their role in a relationship when they learn that a woman's auric and radiant bodies are so much stronger than theirs. It's important for the man to be the one to set high standards for the relationship and demonstrate his integrity and dependability. His commitment will provide his partner with a strong sense of security.

Lovemaking

The act of sex is very powerful, energetic, encouraging, inspiring, widens the consciousness, does everything right when it is done with the right intention, the right environment, the right circumstances, and with the right people.

–YOGI BHAJAN

When you have sex with someone you love, the closeness creates intimacy between you. That's because your energy bodies of sensitivity – your auras – merge during lovemaking. If you care deeply for each other, the experience can be heavenly and reinforce your love and commitment. However, if either partner feels negative or disrespectful toward the other, sex can be very harmful.

Men seek rejuvenation and inspiration from women. If a woman is positive and loving, her aura extends and envelops him during sex. This energizes a man and makes him feel very fortunate and supported by her. However, if he has sex with a woman whose aura is weak, it totally depletes his energy. Being intimately involved with a negative or untrustworthy woman can totally ruin a man, undermine his ability to function, and seriously damage his career.

Mending a Man's Heart

Most of the time men are unaware of how much a woman's actions can hurt them. When a woman acts from her animal nature she can seriously provoke a man. If he is overly intent on pleasing her, he won't have a chance of protecting himself. The effect of a woman's betrayal on a man's psyche can be quite damaging and long-lasting. A man should avoid becoming intimate with a woman until he knows he can trust her values.

A man's temperament is so sensitive that even if his lover fantasizes about having sex with another man, it causes a shock to his mind and emotions. If she goes through with it, and then is intimate with her partner, he can barely survive. The auric injury that results can even make him incapable of having sex with her again. A man's potency depends on the mental frequency and strength of a woman's aura – and her aura is weakened by infidelity.

Men who suffer from relationship trauma can benefit from practicing *Kirtan Kriya,* which heals the psyche. The mantra *Sa Ta Na Ma* strengthens the aura and cleanses the subconscious mind by guiding it through the creative cycle of the finite and infinite. Practicing *Sodarshan Chakra Kriya* can also help men overcome the negative effects of the subconscious mind, which make it difficult to let go of the pain of past relationships.

The Power of Woman

by Yogi Bhajan

When a woman conceives any idea it grows and her mind becomes pregnant with that idea. A woman will deliver no matter what the pain. What about men? Men do not have the capacity of conceiving, maturing, and delivering. Men have the idea to "go and get it."

You have the capacity to nurture and deliver. And your effectiveness is in your discipline. There are four points you must know.

The first thing is that you should be your own disciple.

Secondly, you must conquer your mind and act only through the neutral mind.

Thirdly, you must know that every action has a reaction but in your case it is sixteen times more.

The fourth point you must remember is that when you are out there, incomplete and not ready, you are sixteen times more vulnerable than a male.

Remember, man will live with a mistake for the moment, but you will live with your mistakes for the rest of your life. Because woman's mistaken moments are in her aura and arcline. Woman has a double arcline while man has only one, from earlobe to earlobe. Female also has an arcline across her breasts.

Edited excerpts from a lecture by Yogi Bhajan (July 1994)

A Woman's Purity

A woman's purity strongly influences her relationship with a man, so it's important for her to have a strong aura and arcline. Flirting creates holes in a woman's aura, making her vulnerable to the penetrating quality of the opposite sex. A man will romance a woman into bed with fresh flowers and expensive dinners when he's horny – the next day he won't even bring her leftovers.

A man should only show romantic interest in a woman if he intends to be faithful, not just for his momentary satisfaction. Going through rejection repeatedly is devastating to the female psyche. Blending her aura with multiple sex partners makes it difficult for her to maintain her identity and emotional strength.

For a woman, every sexual experience imprints in her aura and arcline. The imprints of the vibratory frequencies of her sexual partners can remain forever, dimming her radiance. In contrast, a woman's vibration remains in a man's aura for only one lunar cycle – 28 days and four hours.

Fortunately, Yogi Bhajan taught two meditations which can clear a woman's aura and arcline of the imprints of her sexual encounters and give her a fresh start: *Sodarshan Chakra Kriya* and *Kirtan Kriya*. These meditations were not given as license to sleep with several partners; the purity of your intention is essential to receive the benefits of any meditation.

Fear of Men

There must be mutual love and respect during lovemaking for a woman to remain vibrant, secure and expansive. If you have a habit of sabotaging your relationships because of your fear of men, practice Long Deep Breathing 31 minutes a day. In time, you will heal the subconscious blocks that prevent you from feeling secure as part of a couple.

The Art of Long Deep Breathing

Most people do not breathe slowly and deeply. If your breath is irregular and shallow you can't help but feel tense and emotional. On average people use only one-tenth of their lung capacity. Long deep breathing will increase your oxygen intake and cleanse your lungs of toxic irritants that can cause infection and disease.

By practicing this technique you can expand your lung capacity eight-fold and gain endurance and patience. Breathing eight times a minute stimulates your pituitary gland to secrete, while slowing down to four breaths a minute stimulates the pineal gland optimally, making you deeply meditative. To learn the art of long deep breathing, find a quiet place to lie down and relax.

ONE
Close your eyes. Observe the natural rhythm of your breath. Do your chest and abdomen expand and contract? When you inhale, how deeply does your breath travel?

TWO
Put your hand over your navel and inhale deeply through your nose only (your mouth remains closed but relaxed). Let your abdomen expand in all directions as if you were filling a balloon with air. If your abdominal muscles feel tight, consciously relax and let them move upward against your hand.

THREE
With each deepening breath, relax your diaphragm and fill your chest, allowing your rib cage to expand in all directions.

FOUR

Briefly hold the breath in, and allow the air to lightly press against the lungs, gently expanding them. Consciously relax the muscles of your face, neck and shoulders.

FIVE

Exhale slowly through your nose, controlling the release from the upper chest, then the ribcage and finally the abdomen. Press the navel point back toward the spine to completely exhale.

SIX

Briefly hold the breath out and allow the lungs to contract. Then inhale again, fill the abdomen, then the rib cage and finally the upper chest. Exhale. Practice for 3 minutes and then observe your breath again; you should notice that it is deeper, slower and more rhythmic.

SEVEN

Once you have gotten the rhythm of breathing deeply, regulate your breath so you are breathing 8 times a minute or 7½ seconds per inhale/exhale. Once you have mastered this, slow down further to 4 breaths a minute or 15 seconds per inhale/exhale.

With practice, you'll be able to slow your breath down at will during yoga and meditation or whenever you feel anxious, fearful or emotional.

Sodarshan Chakra Kriya

Treat this meditative practice with reverence to increase your depth and caliber and establish inner happiness. *Sodarshan Chakra Kriya* invokes the Kundalini energy and gives you vitality and intuition to combat the negative effects of the subconscious mind. It purifies your past karma and the subconscious impulses that block you from fulfilling yourself. It also gives you the pranic power of health and healing.

Posture & Eye Focus: With your chin pulled in slightly, focus your eyes at the tip of your nose. *Do not do this meditation with your eyes closed.*

Mantra: *Wahe Guru* (pronounced **wha-hay guroo**) describes the ecstasy of going from the darkness of ignorance to the experience of the light within.

Breath Pattern: Block the right nostril with the right thumb and inhale slowly and deeply through the left nostril. Suspend the breath as you mentally chant *Wahe Guru* **16 times**. Pump the navel three times on each repetition of the mantra – once on *Wa*, once on *He*, once on *Guru*, for a total of **48 continuous pumps**.

After completing the **16 repetitions** on the suspended breath, release the thumb, block your left nostril with your right index or pinky finger, and exhale slowly and completely through the right nostril. Then again block the right nostril and continue this breathing and pumping pattern.

To End: Inhale through both nostrils and hold the breath for **5-10 seconds,** then exhale completely. Stretch your arms up and shake every part of your body for **one minute** to circulate the energy you have generated.

Time: Start with **5 minutes a day** and gradually build the time to **31 or 62 minutes.** The maximum time to practice *Sodarshan Chakra Kriya* is **2½ hours** a day.

Kriya for the Aura, Positivity & Vitality

(originally called Kriya for the Electromagnetic Field)

ONE
Sit in Easy Pose and lengthen the spine. Place your hands in Gyan Mudra on your knees and do Breath of Fire. Continue for **3 minutes**, then inhale, hold the breath a few seconds, exhale and relax.

TWO   In Easy Pose hold the ankles and begin flexing your spine forward and back. Inhale as the navel moves forward, exhale as it moves back. Keep your head upright. Continue for **3 minutes**, then inhale deeply, lengthen the spine, and hold the breath for a few seconds. Exhale and relax.

THREE

Remain sitting in Easy Pose and press the tip of the right thumb into the navel. Breathe long and deep for **3 minutes**. Then inhale deeply, exhale completely, hold the breath out, and press the thumb firmly into the navel for a few seconds. Inhale and relax.

FOUR

Sitting in Easy Pose, place your hands on your knees and inhale as you lift your shoulders, exhale as you lower them. Continue at a steady pace for **3 minutes**, then inhale and lift both shoulders as high as you can, creating maximum tension. Exhale and relax, allowing all the tension to release.

FIVE

Bring your arms straight out in front of you with the palms facing each other but not touching. Inhale and swing the arms back as far as you can behind you, with the palms facing forward. The arms will drop down as they swing behind you. Exhale and bring them in front of you to the starting position. Continue the exercise for **3 minutes**. Then inhale deeply with the arms held behind you, and hold the breath for a few seconds. Exhale and relax.

SIX

Sit in Easy Pose and lengthen the spine with the eyes slightly open and focused on the tip of your nose. Breathe long and deep while mentally chanting **Wahe (wha-hay)** on the inhale and **Guru (gu-roo)** on the exhale. Continue for **3 minutes**, then inhale deeply, hold for a few seconds, then exhale and relax.

4

The Nature of the Sexes

A man falls in love when he feels the depth of the woman — it gives him the foundation he needs.

Do not fall in love, do not start loving, and do not make all the associations you want to make, if you have not developed your own maturity that you can contain a man. That's a fundamental requirement. Woman who cannot contain a man shall not have a man.

–YOGI BHAJAN

Containing a Man

Realize that there is a young boy in every man. Just as a mother carries a child in her womb, a wife must carry and nurture her husband – not confront him. If you attack a man, his ego will react. Speak to the child in him, "Look what you did – can't you understand, now we have a big problem." He will say, "Oh dear, I really messed up." If you say, "You idiot, what you did was disgraceful," his reaction will be, "You bitch, who are you to judge me?"

Men are grateful to women because they were carried in the womb. They understand the sacrifice it takes for a mother to turn her blood into milk. Psychologically, a man feels his mother will sacrifice for him whenever he needs it – and he sees his mother in every woman – especially you.

Female contains the male; she contains the he.
Woman contains man even in spellings,
why do you not contain them?

–YOGI BHAJAN

It's not in the male nature to ask for help; men need a woman to be sensitive to them and sense when they are having a tough time. They need your support to do what they know they have to do. What they don't need is for you to try to help or talk them out of it. A man's appreciation will be unending if you let him know that you have faith that he *will* succeed.

*A woman has to understand that if she doesn't want to pull him
out of the difficulty nobody else will. Through the thick and thin
of the time a woman not only has to meditate, she has to
concentrate and inspire the male to keep the relationship going.*
                                                        –Yogi Bhajan

Early in our marriage my husband asked me to let him know what he could
do to make me happy. He explained that the last thing a man wants is to
have to be a mind-reader and guess what you want. I relayed this advice to
a friend when she was frustrated with her marriage:

"Talk about what you would *like*, what would make you happy – not what
you want. Telling a man what you want is too direct, too confrontational.
Once you tell him what would make you happy – let it go. It may be something he cannot deliver. Don't make the mistake of thinking that if he doesn't
give you what you asked for, it means he doesn't love you."

Reflecting a Man

Women suffer in relationships when they try to possess a man, but refuse to
reflect the man. The most powerful communication a woman has is reflecting or mirroring a man's light. The sun shines and the moon reflects the light
of the sun; a woman who wants a heavenly relationship will do the same.

A woman can charm a man by creating a magnetic field between them. Her
supportive intention and subtle energy can create a harmonious relationship. A soft vibration and sweet language suit a woman's make-up because
her magnetic field, magnetic projection, and biorhythm are all oval, like an
egg. Between lovers, communication doesn't need to be super-sweet all the
time; you can be direct with a man as long as your intentions are innocent
and graceful.

A man's nature is to growl, and his instinct, like spermatozoa, is to penetrate. He will unconsciously test and provoke you to prove he's in control. If your radiant body is strong it will act as a shield. The protection of your tenth body will allow you to remain neutral – instead of taking it personally or becoming defensive.

In day-to-day conversation, the problem begins whenever a woman has tension in her voice. If you say, "Get me something to drink," it sounds harsh to a man's ears. "Can you bring me a drink?" is medium-soft. Men will be most receptive to, "Honey, can you please bring me a drink?" It is both polite and appreciative at the same time.

Every action has an equal and opposite reaction and this counts doubly if you provoke a man. You won't get his true response; you'll only get his anger. Even if he is gruff, respond politely as you would in any diplomatic situation. If you react and raise the tone of your voice, you'll create an unwanted drama.

So the basic principle is to contain the man,
not contest the man. Understand?

–YOGI BHAJAN

Creative Communication

By nature man is aggressive and woman is subtle. A woman cannot afford to lose her composure and use unsophisticated language in anger or frustration. She has no margin for error in her behavior because men cannot tolerate complaints, sarcasm, screaming or verbal abuse from a woman.

> *The only thing man leans on is your sweet verbalization.*
> *Man doesn't need you physically or sexually.*
> —YOGI BHAJAN

Men never forget that as a young boy their mother's anger felt like an avalanche. As a result they feel they can never trust you, and anything but supportive loving language reinforces their belief. If you speak to a man the way his mother would – telling him what to do, demanding what you want or showing your impatience – your love relationship with that man will never last.

Graceful, creative communication is achieved by having a positive intent, being subtle in your behavior, and using sophisticated, polite language. In conversation with your partner combine grace *and* romance. Without grace, a man will think he can take advantage of you; without the romance, he cannot envision you as his lover.

A man lives for the creativity of a woman's vibration. First, he seeks the approval of his mother, then the love and appreciation of his wife, and finally the affection of his daughter. Everything a man does revolves around pleasing the women in his life. To make a man happy, express your appreciation for all the effort he makes on your behalf. A man can never get enough appreciation.

A man falls in love when he feels the depth of a woman; it gives him the foundation he needs. He seeks a woman he can trustingly confide in at the end of the day. Emotionally, a man may not always know what he is looking for in the relationship, but interestingly, women usually do. When he is upset he needs *you* to talk to, to unload his troubles. He needs to know you will be there for him without judgment.

Unfortunately, a man is not always able to reciprocate and be an empathetic listener when you need someone to talk to. In general men don't like to talk as much as women, except during courtship! It's not that they are not compassionate to your world; they just cannot see the nuances a woman can see. Even when a man is in love he won't listen to you as much as you would like. You feel neglected when actually he is doing his best to create something positive for you, *because* he is in love.

> *There are certain basic natures which you expect out of the man,*
> *and in his psyche and in his psychology, they don't exist. That*
> *does not mean there is no love, there is no honesty, there is*
> *no sincerity, and there is no communication.*
>
> –YOGI BHAJAN

A man of caliber will always provide a woman with secure environments. If he's in love, his instinct is to protect you. If a man challenges your elegance and grace, walk away – he's not looking for a woman to love and respect.

Pillow Talk

by Yogi Bhajan

Man marries a woman for a pillow talk. That is his ultimate need. Without that, man goes insane. He wants to lie down by somebody's side and whisper in her ear. When he is lying down tired on his pillow, he has no defense.

A woman who provides that opportunity with a smile has the man, doesn't matter what else happens. When a man says, "I want to talk to you," you interrupt and tell him you've been waiting since morning to talk to him!

A woman who can listen to a man can have [him] in her hands. Men want to be listened [to.] If you listen, their whole question is solved. Try it sometime. Do me a favor. Tell them, "Did you say that? Can you repeat it?" Oh my God, you'll have him.

Edited excerpts from a lecture by Yogi Bhajan (June 30, 1997)

Kriya for the Aura, Liver & Self-Reliance

ONE-A

Sit with your legs straight out in front of you, spine straight. Then extend your arms straight in front of you parallel to the floor and lean back at a 60 degree angle to the floor.

ONE-B.

Raise the legs as high as possible. Try not to lean back more than 30 degrees. Then slowly lower the legs back down to the floor to position 1A. Continue this up and down motion while chanting *Sat Nam Wahe Guru* for **3 minutes**. The breathing is automatic.

TWO

With the legs straight out, bend forward and grab your big toes. Press hard with the thumbs on your toenails as you stretch forward, gently bringing your torso down toward your knees. Breathe normally for **3 minutes**, then inhale deeply, exhale and stretch down just a little further. Inhale as you come up with your spine straight, holding onto your toes. Exhale, stretch down and forward. Repeat this stretch 2 more times, then relax.

This exercise can remove all the tension in your body.

THREE

Sit on your heels in Rock Pose with your palms down on your thighs. Begin Spinal Flex, whispering **Sat** as you flex your spine and move the navel forward, and **Nam** as you move back. Keep your chin level and your head steady. Continue for **3 minutes**, then inhale, exhale and relax for **1 minute**.

FOUR

In Easy Pose bring your palms together at the Heart Center and lock the thumbs, right over left. Press your entire weight into the palms and focus your mind at the Brow Point. Breathe normally for **5 minutes** and then deeply inhale, exhale, and relax.

FIVE

Still in Easy Pose, move your waist side to side in a rhythmic motion for **3 minutes**, then inhale deeply, exhale completely, and relax.

This exercise cleanses the liver.

SIX

Repeat Spinal Flex in Easy Pose for **5 minutes**, then inhale, exhale, and relax. *This balances the sexual energy.*

SEVEN

In Easy Pose, rest your hands on your knees in Gyan Mudra. Turn your head to the left as you chant ***Sat Nam***, and to the right as you chant ***Wahe Guru***. Continue for **5 minutes**, then sit straight and inhale, exhale, and relax.

Narayan Kriya to Knit the Tears in Your Relationship

Posture: In Easy Pose tuck your elbows into the body with the forearms angled up so your hands are at the level of the Heart Center, chest width apart or slightly wider. The tips of the index fingers touch the thumb tips in Gyan Mudra, and the palms face up.

Eyes: Focus at the tip of your nose with the eyes 1/10th open.

Mantra: *Sat Narayan Hari Narayan Hari Narayan Hari Hari*
Before each recitation inhale deeply and then chant the mantra in a monotone on one breath. The mantra is pronounced:
sat naraayan haree naraayan haree naraayan haree haree

After **11 minutes** inhale deeply, and as you hold the breath, bring understanding, forgiveness, and blessings to heal your relationship; exhale. Repeat twice more.

To seal the effects of this practice, chant *Wahe Guru* for **3 minutes** with your hands on your knees in Gyan Mudra, or relaxed in your lap, right hand over left, palms up. Chant in a slow monotone – *wha-hay-guroo* – giving equal time to each part of the mantra. *Wahe Guru* describes the ecstasy of going from the darkness of ignorance to the experience of the light within.

A Delicate Alchemy
by Dev Suroop Kaur Khalsa

Our situation has a beautiful uniqueness to it – I am very much into Kundalini Yoga and Sikh Dharma and my husband Gary is not involved at all. Prior to meeting him I had a series of not-so-great relationships. Finally I found this great man and we got engaged, around the same time I began my practice of Kundalini Yoga.

As I grew more and more spiritually, I seriously wondered if I had to make a choice between my new yogic lifestyle and my fiancé, who definitely did not want to live in an ashram. It was pretty dramatic for me because I knew this was what I wanted to do myself but I was conflicted because he didn't. I confided in my yoga teacher and she said, "This guy is better than most Sikh men, if I were you I'd marry him."

Encouraged, I asked Gary to go to White Tantric Yoga in Anchorage with me and meet Yogi Bhajan. To my delight he agreed. We were lucky to catch Yogi Bhajan alone on stage. We sat before him, and terrified as I was, I began to explain our story. He interrupted and said, "Okay, okay, I understand," and rattled off our whole scenario with surprising accuracy.

After asking a few questions, he leaned forward and said to us, "The key to a good marriage is understanding."

He turned, and pointing at Gary, told him, "Remember that." Explaining further he said, "It means *to stand under.*" He demonstrated by putting both hands face up, as if supporting something in his hands. I'm not certain why Yogi Bhajan focused just on Gary at that moment as maintaining a state of understanding was certainly important for me as well.

Then looking directly at me, Yogi Bhajan commented, "I would have married him a long time ago." What I also heard was, "What are you waiting for?"

I really needed to hear his confirmation. I didn't know anyone else in our situation – a Sikh and non-Sikh couple. I believe that the dynamic of our relationship has worked because we reflect on that thought, "Am I being mutual?" I suspect my husband applies the advice similarly since we get along so well.

In my early days as a Kundalini Yogi, I enjoyed a pen-pal relationship with Yogi Bhajan. He personally answered every letter I sent, and I saved them all. Once I was so frustrated with my husband that I wrote him for advice, spelling out all my complaints in detail. This time instead of a letter, I received a call from his secretary with this message:

"He wants you to sit and listen, identify every sound you hear, and name every sound."

> "Is that it?" I asked.
> "Yes."
> "Did he say why?"
> "No he didn't."
> "Did he say for how long?"
> "No," she said, "Just do it and call me back in two weeks."

So I sat outside and listened to the buzzing of flies, the blasting of the weed blower, and cars and trucks rushing by. I got into listening without any time-frame. A few weeks later I called her back and reported, "My husband has become a much more pleasant person."

I didn't understand how this exercise would help. I just went on faith, and it made me more intuitive and subtle, and gave my husband the security of knowing I was present for him. It was definitely more effective than complaining or asking him to see a counselor!

To explain it to my students, I say it this way, "A man will quietly take his cues from a woman, just as a flower turns its head toward the sun. Men need the security that a woman is there for them – they can sense it in your vibration. That is what that simple training was all about. The result of sitting and listening was that I became more attentive without having to try."

The basis of everything I teach in my *Naad Yoga* (sound current) workshops comes from that realization. Listening is key in your relationship with yourself, with others, and with your Creator. It helps tremendously not to jump ahead of the conversation and start planning what you want to say. Your partner will appreciate it if you really listen to what they are saying.

One day a guy in my class announced that he was thinking of leaving his wife. He had missed the workshop the evening before when we did the listening exercise. One of the women spoke up and said, "Teach him how to listen."

When I feel disconnected I always go back to that practice of just listening and identifying the sounds. It is also a very effective way to learn to listen to the sound of your own voice while chanting. When you meditate the important thing is to *listen* to the sound current. What you discover is that when you are listening you are not *thinking*; that's the key.

Even with all these lessons, I still found myself annoyed by my husband at times. At one point his grouchiness was driving me crazy. I decided to ask about it during the Q & A session at the summer camp for women – a cozy but very public forum. Gary was working on Yogi Bhajan's ranch at the time. I knew Yogi Bhajan really liked my husband as he would honor him in class and comment to me about him personally.

That night, Yogi Bhajan wouldn't let me get far, "What questions could you possibly have?" he asked. "Your husband is perfect." He protected my husband publicly, and I learned to do the same. In so many ways he trained me to see my husband was a great being, that there was nothing lacking in him.

He taught me to publicly and privately honor my husband.

The icing on the cake came from a dear friend early in my marriage. She told me that Yogi Bhajan had explained that a man needs to know you will never leave him.

"At some point when you are ready, you need to tell him that," she advised. I wondered if I could ever make that promise. Sometimes I felt confined by marriage and entertained thoughts that there might be something better. Luckily, I did remember when the right time came. My husband was going through an especially tough time. I put my hand on his shoulder and said, "I will never leave you." It had taken some time to get to that point, but I was clear with myself and truly meant it.

5

Married in Love

Just one minute of meditative experience
during White Tantric Yoga is equal to
ten years of meditating together.

Without commitment there is no trust, and without trust you cannot experience deep intimacy in your love life. The basics of a good relationship are openness, honesty, and the desire to give up your individuality to merge and become something new, something unique, something that has never been before.

The most important thing you bring to your relationship is commitment, your capacity to carry something to the end, unto Infinity. Commitment is the first step to achieving happiness; it's your promise to be true. Men and women seek intimacy and for that to happen trust must exist. Once commitment is there, trust is established. The lovers' communication and merger that follows brings the fulfillment of marriage.

> *Marriage is to lose yourselves into one another....*
> *Marriage is not "what about me." Me doesn't exist.*
> *I doesn't exist....After marriage WE exist.*
>
> – Yogi Bhajan

Over the years I heard Yogi Bhajan say many times, "Marriage is the carriage that takes you to Infinity." When you find a spiritual teacher or path, you have to commit to a discipline in order to progress. In essence you are committing to yourself, to the truth of your soul. If commitment is a challenge for you, work on your arcline, the electromagnetic body of purity.

Relationships give us the ability to grow because they entail sacrifice. Everything a spiritual path or teacher can give you, marriage gives you, including the opportunity to love, serve, sacrifice, and demonstrate your finest qualities. Marriage is the highest yoga because it tests the strength of your spirit. To test a student, a teacher will give an impossible task. One of the first things Yogi Bhajan did was to arrange marriages!

He once explained to me that his marriage selections were based on the auras of the couple, not their personalities. In our case, we were in India and one day Yogi Bhajan asked Siri Atma, "What about Nam Kaur?" Siri Atma said, "I'll check it out," even though he already had! He asked to join me for the meditation I was doing, and after the third evening he proposed. We were like two 17-year-olds in love, and Yogi Bhajan had fun teasing us.

A relationship with mutual understanding and appreciation is one in which the couple have merged. One of my friends works with her husband in their home business. People ask how they get along being together all the time. I love her answer. "Sometimes we do get on each other's nerves, but there is no one else either of us would rather spend so much time with."

At a party, Yogi Bhajan's lifelong friend gave me some sage advice. He is a scholarly professor with a twinkle in his eyes that exhibits his love of life. "Marriage doesn't really begin until you turn 70. In the beginning it's about love and passion, then you are busy with work and family responsibilities. In your 70s, the relationship becomes companionship in spirit, and you have time to enjoy each other again." Imagine enjoying someone's company that much after 50 years of marriage!

My husband is a physician and is often present during people's most private moments. One of his patients spent the last day of his life exchanging love notes in his hospital room with his wife of 68 years. Another patient was distraught at the prospect of losing his beloved wife. My husband comforted him saying, "Yes, of course you're upset because you aren't 'you' any longer – you're 'us.' " The man reached out, put his hand on my husband's arm and said appreciatively, "You understand."

Try to understand marriage....A new identity comes out of the two and it is forever; it is not only for today and tomorrow. Life comes to an end – but one thing even God cannot take away – the desire to be one in each other.

–Yogi Bhajan

In a Relationships workshop, I explained that marriage is considered the highest form of yoga as well as the hardest. Nodding in agreement one young woman added, "Yes, it is the hardest because there are two egos involved. And it is the highest because you blend two souls to become one, despite your egos."

Merging Two Souls

My parents recited a prayer together every night before bed for *42 years* – starting on their honeymoon! That simple act created union in the psyches of the two to become one. Yogi Bhajan told me that my parents lived in their radiant bodies. I wasn't sure what he meant until years later when he talked about the essence of the radiant body being commitment, innocence, service, and seeing God in all.

> *Let us understand we have no more power*
> *than our own purity. It is purity and piety*
> *that expand the radiant body.*
>
> –YOGI BHAJAN

One of the best things a couple can do to strengthen their relationship is attend a day of White Tantric Yoga. It is so powerful that if you achieve just one minute of meditative experience during White Tantric, it is equal to *10 years* of meditating together.

We seek intimacy, but the fear of being rejected by our partner gets in the way. White Tantric works on the fears we face with our polarity. It lifts your energy and gives you and your partner a brighter light. During the meditations, the psycho-magnetic fields of the male and female blend to create union of their souls.

[In White Tantric Yoga] you lock in the aura and you lock in the arcline and you lock in all ten bodies and you push through.
                                                                    –YOGI BHAJAN

Couples practice White Tantric Yoga in a group, only under the guidance of the Mahan Tantric, Yogi Bhajan. Using his subtle body, Yogi Bhajan directs the tantric energy, and his recorded instructions are played onscreen. Generally there are six to eight meditations, either 31 or 62 minutes long. Each has a different *mudra* (hand posture) and *mantra* (affirmation) set to music. In most postures you sing, in others you meditate silently.

It's ideal to do White Tantric with your partner, but if you are single or your partner cannot attend, it is still very beneficial. While there are no prerequisites for participating, it is recommended that you attend Kundalini Yoga classes beforehand. Couples will enjoy a deep and sometimes challenging experience. Spending the day looking into each other's eyes – the windows of the soul – will deepen your connection.

Marriage is an exalted state of consciousness where two people practice to become one divine being.
                                                                    –YOGI BHAJAN

Yogi Bhajan's Wedding Advice

Just before we were married on June 26, 1987, my husband and I received a letter from Yogi Bhajan that read:

"June 26th is a very joyous day. My prayer is that you may keep the joy going and growing. Each step taken is a step closer to the Godliness in you. May your steps be as one. May your hands lock together to hold your spirit in *cherdi kala* (high spirits). May your marriage be your carriage unto Infinity. I love you very, very much. Be the leaders unto your own right. Your biggest job is to uplift and inspire others to live consciously. You will be blessed. Take your pain and your weakness to your altar, and give your strength to each other."

Siri Krishna Kaur & Sat Bir Singh Khalsa, Charlottesville, VA

Our Marriage is Stronger
After the Impossible Became Possible

by Tommy Rosen (Bhagat Singh)

Back in 2003, my girlfriend Kia and I decided to go to Maui to celebrate my 36th birthday. We had been together for three years, long enough to know we had something special. We had spoken about the possibility of getting married someday, but I was quite happy to continue on as things were. The convention of marriage, as I had witnessed from my parents and most adults I had known, was fraught with difficulty and challenge. When occasionally I would meet two people who seemed to be doing well together, I relegated them to a special group of human beings who were blessed, but whose lives I could not understand.

Our week in Hawaii was magical and blissful. I could not remember a time when I felt so free of concern. I was overcome by a profound sense of love for Kia and on the spur of the moment I asked her if she would marry me. Our wedding took place two weeks later in Yosemite Valley. Kia walked radiant and smiling through a beautiful meadow toward a life with me. My heart cracked open. For that day and many days thereafter, I knew no fear, no worry and no concern. Later, when life returned to normal and things were not feeling quite so clear and carefree, I remembered the old adage, "Any fool can have a successful wedding." Kia and I had taken a big leap of faith, but I didn't yet know how to have a successful marriage. We were going to need help to make it work.

Two years later, I am facing Kia seated on the floor of a structure known as "the Tantric Shelter" at Ram Das Puri in New Mexico. I am dressed in white clothing and my head is wrapped in a white turban. I am appallingly tired from the past several days of early morning *sadhana*. I sit in a straight line of men, dressed similarly, who are facing a line of women. I see the smiling face of my wife. Our knees are almost touching; our eyes are about three feet apart. This is our first day of White Tantric Yoga. For the next 10 hours we will be engaged in meditations that are physically and mentally challenging. The questions running through my head are: "What are we going to be asked to do? Will I be able to keep up? How did it come to this?"

The promise of White Tantric Yoga is compelling. It is my understanding that, simply put, through this extremely powerful and difficult practice you cleanse your subconscious at the deepest level, of all insecurity and childhood trauma. Who doesn't need a little bit of that?

Staring into your partner's eyes as you perform difficult kriyas is an intense experience. Whatever comes up for either of you becomes a part of the experience for both of you. Many times throughout the day, I would nod off. I tried hard to stay awake, but after a certain point I just couldn't help it. My eyes would roll back for a few seconds and when I came around, Kia would be glaring at me. With her eyes she kept telling me to "pull it together," but the harder I tried the worse it got.

Finally, we came to a *kriya* where we placed our palms against our partners' palms and alternately pushed one hand forward and one hand back. I was frustrated with Kia because she was pushing too hard. She was frustrated with me because I was not pushing the way she wanted. So there we were, one minute into a 62-minute meditation and I was thinking, "This could be the longest hour of my life." And it was! We were yelling using only our eyes and facial expressions – it must have been quite a sight.

When the *kriya* was over, we noticed that several couples were very riled up. What had happened? Issues such as power, control, compassion, patience, and tolerance all came up. You might say it was made to bring up those issues. I had never seen Kia demonstrate intolerance or a lack of compassion toward me. And Kia had never heard me call her a "stubborn goat" before. I remember looking at the enormous photo of Yogi Bhajan on stage and feeling like he was laughing at me.

Kia and I came through our first day of White Tantric Yoga feeling like two embattled boxers. We apologized to each other and committed to do better. The next day, Kia was much warmer, more understanding. I was more patient and more present. One exercise included interlocking fingers with our partner with our arms up at a 45-degree angle. I felt that to make it all the way without lowering our arms would be impossible, but was determined to give it a try. As the 62 minutes passed, a plethora of internal voices rose up and demanded that I lower my arms, but I would not. Kia was right there with me! When the *kriya* was finished, we had completed something that seemed impossible. The power of achieving something you think you cannot do is transformative. That very experience lies at the heart of White Tantric Yoga for me.

Many people have asked what effect White Tantric Yoga has had on my life. I explain it like this: Have you ever been in a place where the background "white noise," such as an air-conditioner or fan, was suddenly turned off? You may have spent months living with that noise and barely noticed it. Now that it's gone, the relief you experience is huge. It feels as if you can take your first deep breath in a very long time. After White Tantric Yoga the garbage of my subconscious, which used to drive so many thoughts and decisions, was removed. My marriage with Kia has gotten better every year because my relationship with my highest self has been able to develop. White Tantric Yoga has made that possible.

Author's Note: White Tantric Yoga® should not be confused with black tantric or red tantric yoga. Black tantric directs the energy to manipulate others and red tantric is solely for sexual purposes. Only White Tantric Yoga®, which purifies the energy between male and female psyches, is part of the science of Kundalini Yoga as taught by Yogi Bhajan™. It is only practiced in the courses offered worldwide by trained White Tantric Yoga® facilitators. You can find the current schedule online at www.WhiteTantricYoga.com.

Creating Intimacy

*There's no relationship which has no sacrifice in it. And there's
no sex which does not make the sixth sense very evident to both
parties. And sex and relationship and love, and whatever
you call it, has three things in it only: trust, trust, and trust.
If you have lost your trust, you have lost everything.*

—YOGI BHAJAN

For true merger to occur a couple must conquer the fear of divulging their innermost selves. It helps to create a nurturing environment to allow this expression. In leading workshops on creating loving and committed relationships, we include topics for couples to discuss. It's wonderful to see the coziness created as they open up to each other and sit closer and closer whispering their intimate answers. One woman said afterwards that her husband of 12 years told her things in class that he had never confided before!

If your partner is willing, pick a time when you will have a few uninterrupted hours, or do a few exercises at a time. Once both of you feel more secure, understood, and loved, your relationship will become more intimate. The goal is to meet each other's needs. Communication takes the guesswork out of it.

ONE

What a man needs from a woman is social protection; what women need from men is personal security. Discuss one issue of this sort that you've been keeping to yourself or that is unresolved. Examples: A man may feel the need to confide in his wife and know that what he shares is just between the two of them. Or he might want to discuss office politics to get his wife's perspective. A woman may worry about the future if the couple does not have adequate savings for retirement. Or she may be concerned that he will find another woman more attractive than her.

TWO

The next step is to identify and write down the following:

Five things that are working well between you
Ten things you've worked on that are resolved or well underway
Two issues you'd like to fix in your relationship

Give yourselves 15 minutes to make your list together. Then decide which of the two issues to work on and discuss for 5 minutes how to move one step forward. The key is not to figure out how to make it perfect, just how to make an improvement. Check in with each other in two weeks to see if your solution is working or if you need another approach.

THREE

When a man really wants to compliment a woman he doesn't tell her she is sexy or pretty. He tells her she is graceful or noble, because those are timeless values. In this exercise, tell your partner which virtue you most appreciate in yourself, and then what you most appreciate in each other.

First the man says what he values most about himself,
Then the woman says what she values most about herself,
Then the husband reveals what he values most about her,
And the wife says what she values most about him.

FOUR

Communicate one thing you would most like to hear your partner say more often and begin doing so sincerely, lovingly, and playfully. Continue for a week or so until you are ready to hear something new.

FIVE

Give each other a 15-minute mini-massage. Let your partner know if you prefer to have your head, feet, ears or hands massaged. You'll be surprised just how relaxing a short massage can be. Make this a habit once a week.

In a loving relationship, there is always a pulsating flow toward sex and intimacy taking place. Sex begins outside the bedroom by feeling secure with each other, and being understood, nurtured, and loved. This creates a cozy environment for sex to take place.

SIX

Explain to each other how you would like to transform yourself in the next few months and how your partner can support you in doing so. Looking at the future and what each person wants to become will help you understand each other's dreams. You may have very different goals, so sharing them and supporting each other will help you remain close.

Now for the really fun part:

SEVEN

Describe what you notice when your partner is in a romantic mood. After you have both done so, tell each other what you think they are *thinking* when they do or say these things. Lastly, reveal to your partner what you *are* thinking when you're in a romantic mood.

EIGHT

For the final exercise, tell each other what time of day you most like to have sex, and then describe what your partner does best in bed. Even couples who have been married for years are surprised by the answers!

Recharge Yourself

ONE

Come into Cat-Cow kneeling on your hands and knees. The arms are straight, knees shoulder width apart. Inhale and drop the spine down as if someone were sitting on your back, and lift your head, being careful not to compress your neck. Then exhale and round your spine up as you lower your head, dropping your chin toward your chest. Keep your eyes closed throughout. Continue the movements with Breath of Fire for **1½ minutes**.

TWO

Sit in Easy Pose and reach your left arm straight out in front. As you twist your torso and shoulders, bring your left arm back, bending the elbow, and bring the right arm straight out. Continue vigorously, twisting left and right for **3 minutes**.

THREE

Come onto your stomach, reach back and firmly grasp your ankles. Pull up on the ankles to bring your chest off the floor. Lift your head and neck, being careful not to compress your neck. Rock back and forth on your stomach in Bow Pose and do Breath of Fire for **3 minutes**.

FOUR

Slowly stand up with your arms straight out in front of you, palms down. Keeping the arms in position, sit down in Easy Pose and stand up again **20 times.**

FIVE

Sit in Easy Pose with your head and neck straight. Bring your arms straight out to the sides, palms up and then raise them overhead and bring the palms together. Holding the position, chant your favorite Kundalini Yoga mantra for **2 minutes**. Inhale and stretch up, exhale and relax the arms down.

SIX

Lie down on your stomach, head turned comfortably to one side, and sleep for **11-21 minutes**.

Long Ek Ong Kars
for Couples

This is a meditation to develop your relationship as a married couple – the state of being as two bodies and one soul.

Posture: Sit in Easy Pose facing each other, knees touching. Hold your partner's hands in Bear Grip (fingers hooked into your partner's fingers). The woman's left palm faces up and her right palm faces down. Look into your partner's eyes and project love and divine light.

Mantra: *Ek Ong Kar Sat Nam Siri Wahe Guru* which means:

 One Creator created this Creation; Truth is His Name and our identity.
 This wisdom is so great it is beyond description.

You can hear the mantra (also called the Adi Shakti Mantra or Morning Call) chanted online at www.kriteachings.org in the Tools for Students & Teachers section under Kundalini Yoga Mantras.

Chant long **Ek Ong Kars** in the 2½ cycle breath:

Ek Ong Kar is chanted in one breath. Pull the Navel Point in slightly on **Ek** (rhymes with neck), a short but powerful sound. **Ong** is a short "oh" with a long "ng" vibrated in the nasal cavity. There is no break between **Ong** and **Kar**, which are equal in length, and the "k" is soft, almost like a "g."

Inhale deeply again and chant **Sat Nam Siri.** Pull the Navel Point in slightly on **Sut** (rhymes with but), a short sound. **Naam** (rhymes with mom) is very long, and **Siri** (sounds like city with a rolled "r") comes with the last bit of breath.

Take a short half-breath to chant **Wahe Guru**. Pull the Navel Point in slightly on **Wa**, a short sound. **He** (hay) and **Guru** (guroo with a rolled 'r') are equal in length.

Time: Continue for **11 minutes**. Then close your eyes and suspend the image of your partner at your Brow Point.

This meditation can also be done sitting back-to-back with your partner with your hands in Gyan Mudra on the knees.

Meditation for Marital & Financial Stability

This meditation is for self-healing, for marital stability, for green energy to come, and for worldly things to lift your spirit. It also helps if you are dealing with another's mental problems. This is a *sarasabud kriya* – it corrects everything.

Mudra: Sit in Easy Pose with your hands in Buddha Mudra – right hand over the left, thumb tips touching. Place the hands against the solar plexus.

Eye Focus: Concentrate at the Third Eye Point and inhale to chant the mantra in one breath. Inhale after each cycle of the mantra and begin again. Radiate a healing aura by mentally projecting green life and green light from your Third Eye. The time is open.

Mantra: *Haaree Haaree Haaree Haaree Haaree Haaree Har*
Haree calls upon the Creative energy and *Har* joins the God within and without.

Commitment is that character you
build in yourself, which is flawlessly
in service of the other.
–Yogi Bhajan

6

Living in Harmony

A woman's charm is to combine
her wit and intelligence in conversation
with the opposite sex.

How can two people live together, talk, and not quarrel?
The arc body and eyesight must connect to feel you want
to communicate with someone. This is where a relationship
is created – psyche-to-psyche.

–Yogi Bhajan

It is painful the way couples talk to each other at times. It's so easy to react and say things we later regret when we feel attacked. But remember that the vibration of every word you speak is a mantra which has long-reaching effects.

Men are very sensitive to a woman's projection – the way you think and feel about him. If you are in the habit of internally critiquing your partner he will sense it. Instead, project that you will love and support him no matter what. You have sixteen times more influence to improve your relationship just by changing your thought projection.

A woman's wisdom is in molding a situation
and not creating a confrontation.

–Yogi Bhajan

The roles of problem-solver and provider define the male identity in relation to women. Men are taught to be providers; it is unacceptable to them not to be. If you tell a man about a problem, his nature is to come up with a solution for you. So when he comes home from work give him time to unwind. Put your pressing issues on the back burner so he doesn't feel obliged to take on more work when he's tired.

Demanding too much when a man is out of energy is a mistake, as is insisting on talking when it's obvious he doesn't want to. Sometimes a woman pushes too hard and finds it hard to backtrack. At that point it's best to let him vent his frustration without getting defensive. Don't prolong the discussion; it will only add fuel to the fire.

If you know how to cover a man in social and financial situations, your relationship will flourish. Your husband may feel provoked in conversation and say the wrong thing. If you step in and say something light and humorous you can save the day. Or perhaps your finances are tight and it's your anniversary. You can creatively produce a beautiful celebration that doesn't involve spending a lot.

Most women have a natural talent for knowing how to create a harmonious situation. A man may not ask for help, but will certainly appreciate it if you pick up the ball when needed. If you fail to do so, he may not complain, but he'll vent his frustration by picking on you later about other things. Subconsciously he may feel you have undermined the relationship because it would have been so easy for you to cover the gap.

Your positive intention can create a new dynamic between you. To change your patterns so your aura can envelop your partner with positive energy, practice the *Kriya for Aura, Positivity and Vitality*. You can also effectively use your body language – smiles, eye contact, laughter and touch – to deliver your message better and faster than anything you can say.

How to Stay "Married in Love"

Q: How can I interest my partner in becoming spiritual?

Nam Kaur: This is a common question women have and more and more men as well. I interpret it to mean, "I'm changing as a result of doing yoga and meditation, and I wish my partner was on the same path." I agree it is nice to share the same path, but just because someone does yoga, it doesn't mean they'll change in the same way or at the same rate as you. I wouldn't judge how spiritual someone is solely based on whether or not they do yoga or meditation – I would look at the purity of their heart.

Q: My husband constantly criticizes me, especially when he first comes home from work when I am most eager to see him. What can I do?

Yogi Bhajan: "Your husband or wife comes home. Their mood is off; they are tired, itchy, angry. At that time, don't start kissing them. First receive them, acknowledge them, sympathize with them. Create the communication, and then say 'I love you.' Otherwise you are creating a war. "

> *Drinking 32 ounces of celery juice a week can*
> *help prevent frequent arguments.*
>
> –YOGI BHAJAN

Q: What can a man do to prevent a fight with his wife?

A: Yogi Bhajan taught that subconsciously your wife wants you to be neutral and steady like the sun. If you let a woman get under your skin, the game is lost. If she is trying to provoke you, do not react. If you feel a fight is imminent, avert it by saying, "Let's discuss it in the morning." The "us" in "let's" will suggest togetherness to a woman.

Q: Ever since we had a big fight my husband virtually ignores me. How can I inspire him to pay attention to me and tune into me more often?

Nam Kaur: Just asking for "attention" is so vague to the male brain that your husband may get frustrated and think he can never meet your needs. Ask for something specific, perhaps time to enjoy a mutual hobby. Tell him you miss him and would like to spend time together, and have a few suggestions in mind. My husband loves to drive so when I want to spend time with him I suggest we explore a new area.

Siri Atma Singh: Sometimes men just need time with other men, or to work out, or to zone out and do nothing (or things their wife might consider "doing nothing"!) They are not like women who love to talk about everything in detail.

If you really want more attention, initiate love-making. Men enjoy being seduced. They don't always want to be the one to ask as it makes them feel they are pushing themselves on you. Even if your sex life is exciting, *make the first move more often.*

Q: When men and women approach middle age sometimes they experience a decline in sexual desire. How can this best be dealt with, both physically and emotionally?

Yogi Bhajan: "Sit together back-to-back and do *Sat Kriya*. Centuries of experience have proven couples remain together, very successful. It is also useful for couples going through calamities, indifference, and unstable environments." See page 117 for instructions.

Q: How can I get my husband to open up to me?

Nam Kaur: If he is willing, do the *Creating Intimacy* exercises together (see page 62) In general, don't question him directly; bring up issues you'd like to discuss indirectly. For example, "My friend told me about this problem with her husband and the way they resolved it was really smart." Your husband can comment on the solution or come up with a better one.

Woman who can involve the ego of the male is successful.

–YOGI BHAJAN

Q: We have been married 27 years. I do not like my husband much any-more, but I still love him. What can I do? He refuses to do yoga or meditate with me.

Nam Kaur: In order to turn the situation around, re-think your internal pro-cess. Your husband may never be inspired to do yoga or meditate, just as you may never share his interests, but your changes can re-inspire the re-lationship. Kundalini Yoga makes you radiant and releases stress, so share your smiles and laughter. Treat your husband as you would a guest in your home. He is sure to appreciate it, and you will avoid the mistake of taking him and your marriage for granted.

A woman who does not ride the ego of the male
is always asking for trouble.

–YOGI BHAJAN

Q: What does it mean to "ride the ego of the male"?

Nam Kaur: Enjoy your husband's expression of himself when he shares his thoughts and feelings. Even if he is angry or upset, let him get it off his chest. Ride his emotions and your reactions, but don't agree or disagree. Listen, nod, smile, understand. Don't stop his flow and add your opinion, especially if you disagree. This will only be seen as a put-down and he will clam up. Wait and give your suggestions later, but don't pressure a man to respond even then.

When you find a good time to voice your opinion, use humor to avoid con-fronting his ego. If he wants to buy a new car and you can't afford one, jokingly say, "Okay, let's get the new car and give up eating!" If you reply with irritation, he'll hear his mother telling him he's no good. If you reply with sarcasm, he'll lose his temper. If you gracefully state the obvious, he'll understand that you feel the two of you are in it together.

Humor

Part of a woman's charm is to combine her wit and intelligence in conversation with the opposite sex. It's your best defense when dealing with problem areas with the man you love. Humor always helps me remain positive when I feel impatient or frustrated. My husband once complained about something I didn't do perfectly for him. Luckily I caught myself before saying something argumentative. I looked at him and said lovingly, "Hey – what about the thousands of little things I do get right?" He smiled appreciatively and we laughed together. Knowing that it means a lot to him, the next time I will make the extra effort.

I made him laugh and bounced back his criticism with the shield of my radiant body, instead of taking it personally. Speaking with a soft voice had the desired effect. The reason he brought it up was because he felt I didn't care about him. Smiling, laughing and being sweet proved I do. I was able to switch gears easily and act playful because my breath rhythm was deep. If my breath had been shallow, I might not have remained neutral. Defending myself would only lead to a fight.

Utilize Your Breath

Breathing deep is a big favor to yourself and your partner. Make it a habit to check your breath throughout the day, especially if you feel uptight. It only takes a few moments to bring your emotions under your control by slowing down the rate of your breath. You'll automatically feel better and maintain your cool.

For instructions on *The Art of Long Deep Breathing* see page 28.

Sweet Talk

Don't overrate the impact of how you speak to your partner. The effect of your words goes deeply into a man's psyche. You can never win if you scream or swear, get pushy or give long sermons. A shrill or high-pitched tone of voice is a definite turn-off – men find it very emasculating.

A tense tone of voice never does any good; it's like a warning signal to a man. His "hearing aid" goes off the moment you pressure him to get your way, so you are wasting your time anyway! All you will end up with is insult. The best way to avoid a fight is to keep the tone of your voice soft and your words polite.

> *What does politeness do for a woman biologically?*
> *It keeps you young and healthy. Polite language*
> *gives your skin all the vitamins you need.*
>
> –Yogi Bhajan

Meditation for Speaking Consciously

Posture: Sit in Easy Pose with the spine straight. Relax your hands on your knees in Gyan Mudra. Your eyes are closed or 1/10 open.

Mantra: Chant in a quick steady pace, like a heartbeat:
>   *Maa maa maa maa maa.*

The breath sneaks in as needed to create a continuous chant.

Focus: Concentrate through the Brow Point – the sixth chakra – so you can command your speech.

Time: Up to **11 minutes**

Benefits: This meditation is very self-nurturing. Your lips may tingle from the stimulation of the mantra. Feel the movement of your lips and consciously hear the sound you create as you enhance your speech and brain function.

Let It Be

If your partner is in a mood where nothing you do satisfies him and it seems a fight is inevitable - let him be. Period. When a man is in that mood, it's just him, his ego, and his frustration. You might as well not exist, and all attempts to connect will be seen as nagging. Remain in your neutral mind to dissipate the tension in the air. A tranquil projection will go a long way.

Nurture Your Partner

When a man works hard his nervous system gets overloaded which puts him on edge. If he acts grouchy, it's easy to take offense and feel hurt. What he really needs at that time is your assurance that you love him and take care of him. Do something special to make him feel appreciated and nurtured – fix a delicious meal, give him a foot rub, or plan a special night for the two of you.

Foot Massage

All the nerve endings in your body end in your feet, so a foot massage relaxes every part of you. If your partner is emotionally weighed down, a good foot massage will do wonders to lift his or her spirits. Massaging the hands will fine-tune and adjust the physical body.

Healing Hands

These exercises will bring more prana – life force – into your hands. Practice **11 minutes** a day to gain the ability to transfer healing energy to someone or something, such as massage oil or a glass of water.

ONE
Rub your palms together briskly for **3-5 minutes** to produce heat in your hands.

TWO-A

Stretch your arms out to the sides parallel to the floor, palms up, thumbs pointing back, and do Breath of Fire for **3 minutes**.

TWO-B

Inhale and hold the breath. Keep the arms out and bend your wrists so your palms are facing out, as if you were pushing walls on either side of you. Feel the energy in the center of your palms flow to your entire body. Exhale and relax the breath.

THREE-A
Rub your hands together
again for **2 minutes**.

THREE-B
Then bend the elbows, keeping your forearms parallel to the floor, left hand
in front of the diaphragm, palm up. Place your right hand palm down, 8"
above the left hand. For a few minutes meditate on the exchange of energy
between the palms of your hands.

Communication by the Stars

Yogi Bhajan gave guidelines for the best time to talk to a man (not just your partner, any man) based on which faculty of nature affects their astrological sign.

If your boyfriend or husband is an earth sign – a Virgo, Taurus, or Capricorn – it's best to talk to him when he is on the move – go walking or hiking together. Never confront him face-to-face.

Fire signs – Leo, Sagittarius, and Aries – enjoy discussion most while they are eating. If you wait until after they eat, they are on to something else and you've lost them.

Men born under air signs – Gemini, Libra, and Aquarius – are most responsive when they wake up – "at first breath." Try discussing things with an air type in the afternoon and he'll be a bear!

Water signs – Pisceans, Cancers, and Scorpios – are most approachable when they say they're happy. Try to engage them at other times and you'll be swamped. If they rarely say they are happy, try asking what would make them happy.

Timing is everything – especially with men. I am always trying to find the right time to discuss things with my husband. If I rule out when he is involved in something, tired, stressed, on his way to work, relaxing after a long day, or recuperating from the work week – there's never a good time! I've had pretty good results talking to him when he is eating, as he's on the cusp of Sagittarius.

Relaxation Series to Remove Negativity & Tension

ONE

Lie on your back and quickly raise and lower your buttocks, creating an invigorating massage to open up the pelvic area. **2 minutes**
Stimulates the juncture of the two sciatic nerves, which is needed for the pituitary to function optimally.

TWO

Remain on your back, arms along the sides of your thighs, feet together. Keeping your head relaxed on the floor, press your toes forward and lift your heels 6" from the floor. Hold the posture and breath long and deep for **3 minutes**. *This posture is for digestion and releasing toxins.*

THREE

Still on your back, lift your left leg up 90 degrees and do Breath of Fire for **1 minute**. *This gives you vitality and removes toxins as well. Note: this is done with the left leg only.*

FOUR

Still on your back, keep your body relaxed and lift your head up, chin into chest. Breathe slowly and deeply for **3 minutes**.
This posture helps to eliminate headaches.

FIVE

Lie on your right side and create a pillow for your head with your right arm. Raise your left leg as high as you can and hold it while you breathe slowly and deeply for **3 minutes**. *Note: this is done only with the left leg.*

SIX

Relax for **3 minutes** on your stomach, head turned to rest on your right cheek, hands by your sides, palms up.

SEVEN

Lying on your stomach, reach back and grab your ankles. Pull your feet toward your buttocks, keeping your chin on the floor. Hold for **2 minutes** with normal breathing, then relax.

EIGHT-A

Still lying on your stomach, bring your heels together. Keeping your arms relaxed at your sides, arch up raising the head and chest off the floor as much as possible. Stick your tongue all the way out and breathe rapidly through your mouth for **2-3 minutes**.

EIGHT-B

Gently roll over and deeply relax on your back in Corpse Pose for several minutes. *You will come out fresh as from a deep sleep.*

Kirtan Kriya for Couples to Clear the Clouds

Kirtan Kriya brings emotional balance and healing to your psyche. When practicing as a couple **31 minutes** is the recommended time. Sit in Easy Pose, with your spines touching as much as possible.

See page 18 for complete *Kirtan Kriya* instructions.

One teacher I know does *Kirtan Kriya* with her husband every evening and says it has enriched their marriage. Getting away from the TV and laptops to focus on a higher vibration gives them the experience of being in one line. She looks forward to sitting down with her husband up against her back, and finds it a great way to end the day.

Yogi Bhajan told another friend of mine to do *Kirtan Kriya* back-to-back with her husband "to have the best sex ever." She enthusiastically told me it works! He also taught that couples should meditate together to attract a beautiful soul, so they did *Kirtan Kriya* when they were trying to conceive. All three of their children are extremely radiant.

November Rain
by Hari Bhajan Kaur Khalsa

We pull into the Union 76 station. The wipers come to rest under the ledge of the hood and the engine quiets. The car reeks of wet dog made more pungent by the warm air gushing through the car's heater. Our pants are soaked through from dripping sagebrush and tall grass that wrapped around our legs as we walked the narrow paths of Solstice Canyon.

My husband gets out to fill the tank. We still haven't spoken since our argument along the trail.

> "There just isn't anyone to take my place right now."
> "I know, honey, but you can't go on this way much longer."
> "I can't just leave the community hanging."

I am tired of his complaints, how he wants more time for himself to paint, go camping, travel.

> "It's 10 years now. When is it your turn?"
> "I'm not ready."
> "What about me? How long do I have to wait?"
> "I've got to do it my way, in my time."
> "But, honey…"
> "I don't want to talk about it anymore."

Raindrops rush to settle on the wide expanse of the molded Plexiglas windshield. They adhere to the surface, gyrating and pulsing in primal rhythm. Some can't hold on to the slick surface and skid off the sloping side into the wind. Others trickle down into the engine and sizzle on the hot metal.

Strung over the highway a traffic light careens on a thin, dark line holding the cars and trucks from advancing, then bidding them forward. On the other side of the highway a low-slung, paint-chipped plant nursery is wedged, like a piece of California pie, between Highway One, Topanga Creek and the 50-foot, ochre-colored cliffs that loom behind it. Across the face of the building a white signboard spelling out Cosentino's in hand-painted black letters lurches like a ship in turbulent seas toward the entrance. Lashed to the rooftop, a daffodil-yellow lawn chair and chaise lounge threaten to break from their moors and launch out to sea.

Cradled in my car-cocoon the water spits and reels outside. In spite of it, traffic on Highway One propels relentlessly. A few feet from the road the ocean roars and hurls its foaming talons at the succumbing sand. Topanga Creek flexes the new muscles of its rising waters as it rushes to the sea. Outside my husband in his blue rain jacket, hand on the gas pump, removes his hood and opens his face to the stinging pellets of rain.

He has always been a man of duty, responsibility, the one willing to carry the load. I love him for this but he does not dare to dream that duty and service can co-exist with desire and freedom. He longs for and is terrified to release his passion for fear it will consume him. He looks into the well and sees only darkness.

I float on liquid memories: I am eight, at the top of the soft hill in back of Betsy Johnson's house on Canyon Drive after a night of dry, powdery snowfall with my Radio Flyer poised; I am 17, on a blistering August afternoon, racing across the desert on spotted horses terrified and exhilarated as lightning and thunder crack the cobalt sky; I am 23, clutching his hand, pushing and moaning as tears flow unbidden and the miracle of birth consumes me; I am 41, arms outstretched belly to the sky in the luscious womb of Scout Lake high in the Cascades with the summer sun slipping under my eyelids and the playful shouts of children in my ears.

The driver side door opens and my husband slides onto the seat. He turns the ignition and the needle on the fuel gauge rises to full. Beads of water roll down his jacket and scatter into the air as he pulls on his seatbelt.

I peel my cheek from the window and pull up out of a slump into a sitting position. "Wow, it's really coming down."

> "I love this weather."
> "We were lucky to get our walk in before the deluge."
> "I wish it would rain more."

He switches on the headlights and turns the wiper knob. The giant arm rises from its cave and wipes the glass bare. Before it completes its arc the drops begin to fill in the empty space. Each perfect sphere makes room for the other on the glass. If one is lost, another immediately fills its place. We idle at the edge of the highway, waiting to pull into the splashing corridor between sea and crumbling hills.

He points at Cosentino's as he turns the wheel right and joins the traffic flow. "Isn't that the place that was almost washed away in the floods a few years back?"

> "The creek overflowed. It was the first time in fifty years."
> "It's amazing how some things survive through all sorts of disasters."

He turns to me with a boyish glint in his eyes.

We travel the highway back to Los Angeles winding along the farthest edge of the continent with the Pacific Ocean stretching to the gray horizon. He focuses on the road and the job before him. His courageous and gentle nature washes over me. I see the ocean, the mountains, the forests and wind cascading through his being. Just as this ribbon of road cannot keep the rainwater from reaching the sea, so I am sure that fear is no barrier to his desire to fulfill the promise of his soul. His answers will arrive just as the rains fall – in their own time, in their own rhythm.

The car accelerates as we hit the Santa Monica freeway. The dogs tuck their feet a little tighter into their chests. The leather of the car seat hugs my damp body. We are only minutes from home and a hot bath.

Conflict is a part of life whether among nations, neighbors, marriages, or within our own minds and, though often painful and confusing, it is an essential element for transformation. We are always in relationship to conflict and in relationships there are always choices. Our choices lie in how we perceive the conflict, what avenues we turn to resolve it, and how we handle the outcome. We can either react or respond. When we react we confront conflict at the level of fear. We are compelled to impose our solutions, our beliefs, our answers on those around us. We use weapons, words or energy to force the outcome in our favor.

When we respond in consciousness we call upon qualities of patience, awareness and love to aid us in unraveling the elements of the conflict and illuminating our decision making. The broader and deeper our powers of contemplation and discernment the more likely a place of peace and clarity will be found.

It is in this process of inner dialogue that the path is born for our response to conflict. We have the choice to impose our will on the conflicts before us or, as a flowing river bends in its course, we can embrace our challenges and allow ourselves to be transformed.

Once a word comes out, beyond the teeth, it's an arrow which has left the bow. It cannot come back. It may miss its target, but it will get somewhere. It may not give the interlock impact which you want. Consciously it may not hurt, but subconsciously it will live. Unconsciously it will become a reminder to the other person.

–YOGI BHAJAN

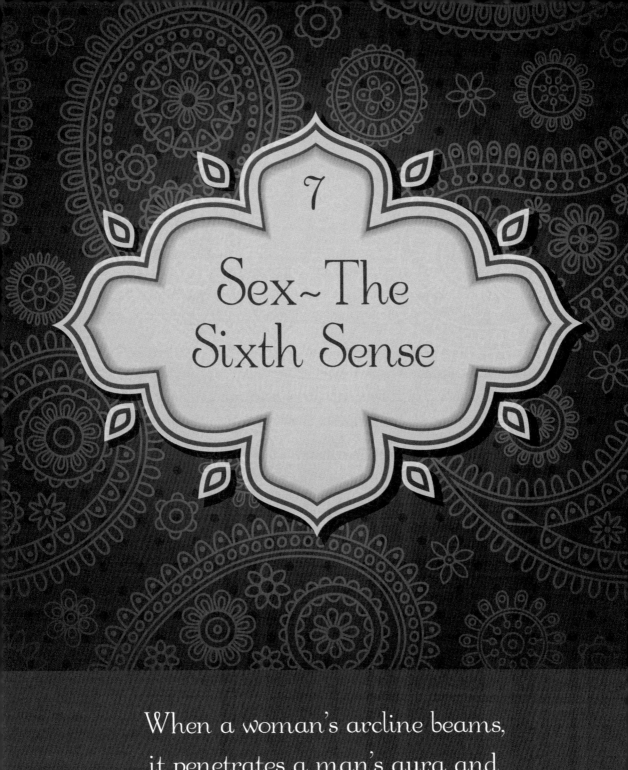

7

Sex~The Sixth Sense

When a woman's arcline beams,
it penetrates a man's aura and
stimulates his pituitary gland.

When you are in love, neither you hear, speak or see – all five senses have one sense of ecstasy....The total amalgamation of these five senses is the sixth sense or the sex sense.

–YOGI BHAJAN

Sex can be divine, and if done with purity of heart, it strengthens your connection as a couple. During intercourse the outer edges of your auras blend and become one. When you have sex in this interlocked state of higher consciousness it regenerates your body and rejuvenates your psyche. The intuitive energy created by the sixth sense is very powerful and gives you the creativity to achieve and succeed.

The Trigger for Sex

Your longing for romance and love, your desire to have intercourse, and your potency are all based on the biorhythm of your pituitary, the master gland. Believe it or not, your sexuality is controlled by the pituitary, not the sex organs. Your pituitary acts and reacts according to the pheromones you and your partner produce. This subtle fragrance is what attracts the opposite sex. It is the scent of a woman that entices a man – he imagines coziness and comfort.

It is such a powerful phenomenon that a woman can be attracted by her lover's scent from miles away. Birds can track each other in the sky through the pheromones their wings leave behind as they fly. It was scientifically proven in 1986 that these special aromatic chemicals directly affect sexual physiology.

'When a woman receives the pheromones exuded in a man's body odors – either by smell or skin absorption – they automatically improve her physiological functioning. You might say exposure to pheromones is the essence of sex.'

© Nov. 18, 1986, The Washington Post

A woman's fragrance arises from her Crown Chakra, and can penetrate a man's aura with incredible speed and potency. When her arcline beams, it also penetrates his aura and stimulates his pituitary gland. The trigger for their sexual desire is this interplay between her arcline and his aura.

These days, men and women cover their natural aromas with so many scented products and perfumes that there is no chance for a personal relationship to develop. A man's charm is his freshness. When he is feeling seductive, he should wash under his arms with cold water to remove the exhaust from his brain and keep his pituitary alert. A woman should shower to keep her scent fresh.

Sex for Breakfast, Lunch & Dinner

A well-known Kundalini Yoga teaching is to have sex only once a month. Many have asked if this is a hard and fast rule or was given in the '70s to counter-balance the "free love" era. Since I had never heard Yogi Bhajan say this myself, I also wondered. I personally heard him tell one young woman who was having marital difficulties to "have sex for breakfast, lunch and dinner!" He also jokingly told us we could have sex six times a day if we liked – and he would visit us in the hospital!

I discovered a 1974 lecture where Yogi Bhajan addresses the subject, playfully saying that we believe that if we have a good relationship, we can afford to indulge more than once a month. Sex shouldn't begin under the covers, he explained, but a week before spending time together, building desire with sweet talk and looking into each other's eyes. Then your passion comes into play during four or five hours in bed. You melt into each other and in this sensual and sexual play you are beyond time and space.

It occurred to me that if it takes a week to set the scene for a good sexual encounter, a yogi can indulge four times a month! Yogi Bhajan also said many other times that setting the mood for sex ideally begins three days in advance.

The dance that begins before sex is the dance of getting to know each other anew. If this communication stops taking place, an underlying frustration builds and the joy of sex breaks down. Certain feelings need to be awakened in the male, and especially in the female, in order for them to relax and respond in a truly open way. Ideally what a man needs to do to romance a woman prior to sex is to touch her psyche, not buy her sexy lingerie. He reinforces her awareness of her sexuality and lets her feel his honest love for her.

I'd have to agree that the best sex begins outside the bedroom. Playfulness is a wonderful way to set the mood and heighten desire. Create an atmosphere in which both of you are relaxed and comfortable. It's especially important for a woman, as her ten bodies must all be in the mood for love or it is best to avoid it altogether. A man must realize that he is dealing with ten bodies in one.

Some people think if they avoid sexual relationships altogether they are very spiritual, but without it your inner self loses the essence of life. On the other hand, overindulging for physical satisfaction alone misuses the flow of the spirit. Both are escapism. Engaging in too much or too little sex is unhealthy.

Without love you can never find your life,
and with lust you can never enjoy life.
*—*Yogi Bhajan

Yogi Bhajan taught us the science of cause and effect for every aspect of life and left it to us to decide how to best use our energy. He advised one newly married couple to have plenty of good sex, but to be sure to recuperate afterwards. Luckily he gave us many yogic tips to do so!

FROM HER PERSPECTIVE:

It is very reassuring for a woman to know that her partner is turned on by her body exactly as it is. Once she can relax about her physical appearance she is free to be much sexier with her man. No matter how beautiful a woman's body is, she will never be satisfied unless her partner reaches out to touch her heart and soul. He must long to become part of her. He must open himself to this possibility or she will never be secure in her body image.

Foreplay

Playmate is a very polite wresting match, in which a man and woman induce their integrity, their divinity, their love, their touch, their feeling, their smell and overall, their understanding.

–YOGI BHAJAN

A couple can enjoy a state of ecstasy with spiritual foreplay that involves play, dance, fantasy, adventure, music, massage. Take your time and enjoy the sensations of your entire body as a sexual platform. Involving all the senses will engage the interest of both partners and heighten the experience.

Sexually and sensually a woman must achieve a state of tiding – wave after wave of orgasm. Before penetration, a couple can enjoy exchanging sensual caresses and kisses. To satisfy a woman, a man should give ample time to these ultra-sensitive areas: her hair, lips, cheeks, ears, back of the neck, breasts, navel, lower back and inner thighs. This will arouse her clitoris and vagina. A woman is much more receptive in lovemaking if aroused to the point of tiding.

For a man these areas are key: his head, hair, lips, his entire back from the neck to the buttocks, his navel and inner thighs, as well as the more obvious pleasure spots – his testicles, penis and nipples.

Orgasm

A man who really wants to satisfy his woman will bring her to orgasm before he climaxes. Physiologically it's important for him to arouse his partner long enough to activate her pheromones, so his pituitary is optimally stimulated in the act of love. When a woman's pheromones secrete, her essence changes the man's pituitary by stimulating his sense of smell. Unlike all the other senses, the sense of smell enters the brain unfiltered.

If one of you reaches orgasm before the other, it is crucial that you excite your partner to climax too. Your love life and relationship will remain exciting both in and out of the bedroom if you make this effort. If either partner is left unsatisfied, it can ruin the energy between you and seriously impair your relationship. Men can end up with serious prostate problems if they engage in sex too often without ejaculating.

Passionate Positions

One afternoon sitting by the fireplace with Yogi Bhajan at his favorite hotel in Santa Fe, the subject of sex came up. He leaned in and confided the following: "This position is particularly enjoyable for women – the couple lies on their sides, and the man enters the woman's vagina from behind. He alternates playing with her breasts and clitoris while biting the back of her neck." I immediately wrote it down. He had never been this explicit before about sexual positions, even during his women-only lectures.

Interlock Intercourse

The true act of intercourse is when a woman knows how to interlock a man's penis so firmly he cannot move except to ejaculate. This gives a man immense pleasure, and can also excite women who have trouble reaching orgasm. Having strong Kegel muscles is the secret to enticing a man with your sexual strength. Even if you never master the art of gripping so tightly that your partner cannot escape, you can stimulate him while practicing "Kegels" during sex or after he climaxes.

FROM HIS PERSPECTIVE:

Getting on top of your partner, and facing away from him while interlocking his penis is especially exciting for a man. It is the ultimate way of giving him pleasure because he can be completely taken without having to perform. When you hold a man with the core of your being, he knows without a doubt you will never let him leave you. This is the type of communication a man understands and appreciates.

Strengthening the Kegel Muscles

The easiest way to identify the Kegels – the muscles of the pelvic floor – is to stop and start the flow of urine. Once you've identified them, practice the following exercise when your bladder is empty, either sitting or lying down:

- Contract the Kegel muscles, hold for 5 seconds, then relax for 5 seconds.
- Do this 4-5 times in a row. Work up to holding 10 seconds and relaxing 10 seconds between contractions.
- Be sure you are tightening only the pelvic floor muscles. Breathe freely and avoid holding your breath while you practice.
- For best results, work up to 500 repetitions a day. You don't need to do them all at once. You can do it discreetly anytime, anywhere – you can even do Kegel exercises when pregnant.

Men who suffer from premature ejaculation or who do not produce enough pre-ejaculate to lubricate the urethra, can also benefit from actively exercising the Kegel muscles.

Pelvic Pleasure

One especially satisfying movement for both sexes is when the male is on top and the female circles her pelvis as he penetrates her. This circular motion stimulates a woman's clitoris and captivates a man's imagination. Additionally, it helps prevent the man from putting too much pressure on the woman, which could cause her hip socket or pelvic bone to move out of place during sex.

Formula for Ecstasy

At the height of passion your breath will reach between 21 to 26 breaths per minute – that's the formula for ecstasy. At this time glandular secretion is at its peak and the heat of your breath changes the scent of your bodies. This fragrance is said to keep a man and woman young for months and months.

A man cannot become aroused without a woman putting out the call through her fragrance. It triggers his scent to secrete, which in turn arouses a woman sensually. Once she gives the call she should totally and creatively enjoy the male, and thoroughly drain his juices. A man's primal need is to be emptied and refilled by the essence of the female spirit. Being satisfied creates the ecstasy of openness which draws a man outside himself. Through their merger the woman is satisfied, and knows he is for her.

Prolonging Erection

If a man breathes through his right nostril during sex, he will have a strong desire to ejaculate. Breathing out of his left nostril will allow him to enjoy intercourse longer. To switch nostrils, he can put his hand in his left armpit, apply pressure, and breathe deeply for three minutes. This takes the pressure off, so you can take your time.

Post-Sex Rejuvenation

After you climax, merge into each other by maintaining physical contact and connection. To recuperate after sex, you can snuggle, whisper "sweet-nothings" or give each other mini-massages. A brief head rub can be very relaxing. This is also a perfect time for a man to massage a woman's breasts. It's essential to circulate the blood in the skin around the breasts to keep them healthy. Encourage him to get lost in it for 10 to 15 minutes.

After a satisfying sexual experience, it is natural to want to drift into a blissful sleep. However, falling asleep immediately after sex can weaken your nervous system. The left nostril and the parasympathetic nervous system must become dominant to allow your body to relax and recuperate. You can switch your predominant nostril from right to left by urinating within 15 minutes of climaxing. It's especially important for a man to do so to prevent prostate problems.

While it may seem like too much effort, it's important to take care of a few other things before falling asleep.

Male Maintenance

Ejaculation is a huge energy loss for a man, as it takes 80 drops of blood to make one drop of semen. To recoup the energy lost from ejaculation, men should have a glass of Sesame-Ginger Milk within 45 minutes of climaxing. Sesame-Ginger Milk nourishes a man's nervous system and rejuvenates his sexual organs. It can be made ahead of time and kept by the bedside table. A simple variation is to have a glass of warm milk with a tablespoon of raw sesame oil.

> ## Sesame-Ginger Milk
>
> Blend until smooth:
>
> > 12 oz. milk (dairy, soy, rice or almond)
> > 2 Tbsp. (1-3") fresh ginger root,
> >   peeled and finely chopped
> > ¼ cup tahini (ground sesame seeds)
> > 2 tsp. maple syrup or honey
>
> To serve warm, carefully heat with a table-spoon of ghee (clarified butter) and store in a thermos.

Youth & Vitality for Women

Before a woman has sex, it is beneficial for her to drink a cup of sweetened Yogi Tea. (A man should have his Yogi Tea or Sesame-Ginger Milk *after* sex.) To stay young and avoid taxing her body unnecessarily, she should also adopt the following routine post-sex:

- urinate within 15 minutes to balance her energy

- brush her teeth

- wash the following areas with cold water:
  - her face
  - behind her ears
  - under her arms (to balance her parasympathetic nervous system)
  - the inner thighs
  - her feet

- And lastly, stretch her body to realign her posture with the post-sex stretches that follow

Post-Sex Stretches for Women

Sometimes, improper movement can cause a woman's pelvic bone to move out of place during sex or the angle of her legs can put too much pressure on her hips. Stretching her body with Cat-Cow, Cat Stretch, and Baby Pose before falling asleep will save her a lot of trouble and help prevent hip problems, pain back, sciatica, low energy, and poor circulation in the legs.

Cat-Cow stimulates the main nerves that are regulated through the lower cervical vertebra of the neck.

Cat Stretch stretches the muscles of your entire back and massages the reproductive organs. It releases tension and stiffness, allowing your energy to flow.

Baby Pose brings a good circulatory flush to the brain, eyes and upper glands.

Cat-Cow

Come into Cat-Cow by kneeling on your hands and knees. Position your arms under your shoulders, elbows straight, knees shoulder-width apart. For Cow, inhale and drop the spine down as if someone were sitting on your back, and lift your head, being careful not to compress your neck. For Cat, exhale and arch your spine up as you lower your head, dropping your chin toward your chest. Keep your eyes closed throughout. Start slowly, breathing powerfully, for **1 to 3 minutes**. Gradually increase the speed as you feel your spine becoming more flexible. To finish, inhale into Cow, exhale, and relax.

Cat Stretch

Lie on your back with your arms on the floor overhead. Inhale deeply, bring your left knee up and over your body as you twist your hips to the right and hook your left foot behind your right knee or thigh. Bring the knee as close to the floor as you can comfortably. Keep your shoulders on the floor, and turn your head to the left. Exhale completely as you bring your arm and leg back to the starting position. Switch legs and continue stretching, **10-20 times to each side**.

Baby Pose

Sit on your heels, bend forward and put your forehead on the floor with your arms alongside your body, palms up. Relax the muscles in your neck and shoulders, along the spine, and in your hips and buttocks, by breathing slowly and deeply as you relax into the posture.

Kriya for Nervous System & Glandular Balance

ONE

Sit in Easy Pose with your arms extended straight out to the sides, parallel to the floor. The palms face up. Begin moving only the middle fingers (the Saturn fingers) up and down rapidly. With a powerful breath, inhale as you raise the fingers and exhale as you lower them. Coordinate the movement with your breath for **7 minutes**.

This exercise stimulates the pituitary to create a balance between the parasympathetic and sympathetic nervous systems.

TWO

Still in Easy Pose stretch your arms out in front of you, parallel to the ground
with the left hand over the right. Interlace the fingers with the palms facing
down. Rapidly swing your arms from side to side, moving your head and neck
in the same direction as your arms. Keep the elbows straight. Coordinate the
movement with a powerful breath for **5 minutes**.

*This exercise makes the body very flexible, strengthens the chest muscles and
stimulates the breast tissue and lymph nodes in that area.*

THREE

In Easy Pose, extend your arms straight out in front, parallel to the ground. Make your hands into fists with the thumbs tucked inside touching the fleshy mound below the little finger. Keeping your arms and hands straight, bring the left arm up as the right arm goes down. Continue alternately moving the arms up and down powerfully, coordinating the movement with forceful breathing for **8 minutes**.

This exercise balances the parathyroid gland and stimulates weight loss.

FOUR

Sit with the soles of the feet pressed together in Butterfly Pose. Draw your feet into the groin, keeping your knees as close to the floor as possible. Interlace the fingers and place the hands in your lap. Inhale and raise your arms up over your head while simultaneously drawing your knees up toward the center of the body. Exhale and lower your knees and arms down to the original position. Continue rhythmically, coordinating the movement with powerful breathing for **8 minutes**.

This exercise balances the prana and apana (the eliminating force of the body), sets the navel point, and brings the breast line into balance. It is excellent for a woman's pelvic area, especially during her child-bearing years.

Sat Kriya for Couples

At some point, either you or your partner, or both of you, may experience a diminished desire for sex. This is common among couples approaching middle-age and those with high stress levels. To make a fresh start as a couple, you can do *Sat Kriya* sitting back-to-back with your spines touching. This will stimulate sexual desire and improve the energy between you when going through marital difficulties.

> *Two spines joined together in Sat Kriya can do wonders.*
> — YOGI BHAJAN

Sat Kriya is one of the few Kundalini Yoga techniques that is complete in itself as a kriya. It strengthens the nervous, digestive and sexual systems, heals mental imbalances, and raises the Kundalini – giving you increased vitality and consciousness.

Mudra: Sit on your heels in Rock Pose back-to-back, with your spines touching as much as possible. Stretch your arms straight overhead hugging your ears, with no bend in the elbows. Interlace the fingers with the index fingers pointing up, and close your eyes. Men cross the right thumb over the left, and women cross the left thumb over the right.

Mantra & Breath Pattern: Inhale slightly to begin and powerfully chant *Sat* as you pull the navel in and up powerfully. This will automatically contract the rectum and sex organs as well. As you chant *Nam* release the navel and let the breath go.

Chant in a steady rhythm, **8 times every 10 seconds**. *Sat* is chanted powerfully from the navel point, and *Nam* is barely audible. Don't worry about the breath as it will regulate itself. Keep your chest, shoulders, and arms stationary and put your effort into squeezing the energy from the navel. Relax your face.

Mulbandh & Neck Lock: To end this part of the kriya, hold the position, stretch up, inhale deeply, and squeeze Mulbandh (the navel, rectum, and sex organs). Draw the energy up your spine to the top of your head and fingertips. Hold **8-10 seconds**, then exhale. Repeat once more, then inhale deeply, exhale completely, apply Mulbandh and Neck Lock and hold the breath out a few seconds. Inhale, relax the breath and release the locks.

To Finish: Lie on your back in Corpse Pose for the second part of *Sat Kriya*. The deep relaxation is very important – it allows the energy you generate to circulate and flow from the nerves emanating from the navel to your entire body. Relax for the same length of time as you practice *Sat Kriya*.

Timing: Beginners can start with **1 minute** and build up to doing **3 minutes** a day for a quick tune-up. Slowly increase the time of this powerful practice to **11, 22, 31,** or **62 minutes**, or at most **2½ hours**.

Editor's Note: Yogi Bhajan was not specific about how to do Sat Kriya as a couple, except to say it is beneficial to have your spines touching. Since Sat Kriya is traditionally done in Rock Pose, this would seem the preferred way to do it as the spines touch optimally if one of you puts your toes over the toes of the other. If you sit in Easy Pose, you may find that your lower backs do not touch because of the natural curve of the spine.

8

Sexual Potency

A man should stimulate his lover
long enough for her pheromones to
stimulate his pituitary.

Sex is not in the second chakra. The sixth is the command center (your pituitary), and it's the sixth center that will serve you, not the second.

                                        –Yogi Bhajan

A man may be driven by his passion for sexual release if he is in his second chakra. For sex to be a creative act, it needs to come from the center of creativity. Sex and success are one and the same, and come from the same energy and projection. If a man does not possess sexual pituitary control, his social life, personal life, sex life, family life, and accomplishments will all be 60 percent less satisfying, as his projection will be much weaker.

The pituitary controls your biorhythm which influences your mood. Your mood controls your creativity, and your creativity directly affects your sex life and your success in life. Men become impotent when their pituitary no longer regulates the chemistry of all glandular secretions into the blood-stream. It is the consolidation of these glandular secretions that determine male sexual strength or potency.

When men become impotent they feel miserable, and not just because they can no longer have sex. Your sensory system, the sixth sense, is weak when you are not in good shape sexually, and your pituitary does not work for you. To enjoy good health, your pituitary must create healthy blood chemistry. If it does, even a man in his eighties who is unable to perform sexually can be healthy and vivacious.

Sexual Pituitary Control

When a man is aroused sexually, the prostate gland* secretes in order to oil the male sexual tract (the urethra) before ejaculation. The sexual tract must be alkalized before ejaculation because acidic environments are unfavorable to sperm. Pre-ejaculate neutralizes the acidity caused by urine, creating a safe passage for the neutral sperm. If a man does not produce enough pre-ejaculate he may benefit from exercising the Kegel muscles – see page 106.

When his lover arouses his pituitary to secrete and pulsate, a man gets an erection and is ready to penetrate. Before he does, he must engage in foreplay for a long stretch of time to stimulate his pituitary to signal the prostate gland. Once the prostate secretes urethral gland fluid, the urethral tract is neutralized. A man knows if the urethra has been properly alkalized if fluid (pre-cum) comes out when he presses the tip of his penis.

If the urethra is not adequately alkalized, it means the pituitary has not been adequately primed to accept the pressure of ejaculation. Ejaculating prematurely throws a man off-balance for an entire lunar cycle. His magnetic field is incomplete and his pituitary impaired, so he becomes forgetful and cannot work normally. A man loses two-thirds of his ability to think, project, and create, just by making this one mistake.

* When Yogi Bhajan speaks of the prostate gland in this situation, he is referring to the job of the prostate gland, the urethral or cowpers glands, and the seminal vesicles together. It is common in lay literature to refer to their secretions as "semen" as they share chemical similarities, though differences do exist.   – Dr. Siri Atma Singh

Premature Ejaculation

Men who have trouble maintaining an erection, or who ejaculate prematurely, should actively exercise the Kegel muscles. This will also help produce the necessary pre-ejaculate to lubricate the urethra prior to penetration.

Male Maturation

Males mature sexually between the ages of 12 and 21 to 24. During this time a young man's semen circulates through the spine to the brain repeatedly. This is essential for the proper timing to be established between the testicles and the pituitary gland. If this process is disturbed by ejaculation the brain is unable to do its job; if uninterrupted through the age of 24 (i.e., no sexual intercourse or masturbation), a young man's semen will be golden-brown and fragrant like sandalwood.

> *First 18 years pituitary supports you 100 percent;*
> *next 18 years it supports you marginally; and then*
> *you are on your own.*
>
>   –YOGI BHAJAN

What this means is that until you are 18 years old you are full of stamina; between 18 and 36 your potency declines and you should develop discipline; and after age 36, without discipline, you have nothing to cover the gap.

If a man doesn't control his sexual desires when he is young – including masturbation and wet dreams – he will pay a heavy price after the age of 54. Overindulging sexually ruins a man's pituitary adjustment and weakens his entire glandular system. This leads to numbness, insensitivity, and impotence. If a young man has the discipline to abstain from sex until he's 25, he will never suffer from weakness or senility, and his creative consciousness and projection will be extremely sharp.

Best Times to Have (and Not Have) Sex

Avoid sex between 3 a.m. and 6 a.m. – the angle of the sun and earth make it a sensitive time of day, best suited for meditation. Avoid sex when you are very hungry, within 3 to 4 hours of eating or exercising, if the woman is deeply menstruating, and when you are under stress. Sex should be avoided if you are in a hurry, worried, or not in a secure place. Any other time when you are both relaxed and you can sleep afterward is fine.

The most detrimental thing is to indulge in sex right after you have eaten, as it can ruin the strength of your digestive system. Men who routinely do this ultimately suffer from premature ejaculation. The majority of male impotency results from poor digestion, as it puts a heavy drain on a man's sexual system.

When you eat, your heart sends blood to the stomach for digestion, and you should be relaxed mentally to digest properly. During sex you are actively in your head. If you eat soon after having sex you seriously overtax your stomach. You cannot light up the pituitary, the digestion, and the muscular system all at once. The heart cannot provide adequate blood flow to all three areas. Your blood chemistry will be impaired and your glandular, digestive, and nervous systems will suffer, aging you tremendously.

Another bad habit is when a man goes on and on having sex and does not discharge. This becomes a problem for those who routinely have sex when they are tired. Eventually the nervous system freezes and the nerves become frigid. It is best for a man to establish the discipline to have sex when he is rested enough to enjoy it and achieve orgasm. If he makes it a habit to get up to urinate within 15 minutes of ejaculating, he can avoid serious problems with his prostate later in life.

In the act of love, a man should stimulate his lover long enough for her phero-mones to activate his pituitary – otherwise it's like masturbation, and all he'll get out of it is irritation. Masturbation is heavy on the brain. It pressurizes the gray matter in the serum and causes a triple action on the pituitary gland, which takes away a man's power to concentrate.

When a man feels horny, he can either meditate to elevate himself or engage in sexual activity. Sexual desire can be transformed to pure creativity by raising the energy through meditation. Once a man's sexual energy moves to his testicles, his aura contracts and he seeks release. The release he seeks is not purely physical – by nature he is a seeder, so he will pursue a female who will nourish him.

Pituitary Gland Series

Under the effects of pressure and relaxation in Triangle Pose, Cobra Pose, Front Bend, Yoga Mudra and more, the pituitary gland secretes and your mind and body are rejuvenated.

ONE Lunge Stretch

Starting in Rock Pose, raise the right knee, and put your right foot flat on the ground. Extend your left leg straight back and place your hands on the floor for balance alongside your right foot. Lift your chest from the heart center and arch your head back, being careful not to compress the neck. Hold the position, breathing slowly and deeply for **1 minute** – then do Breath of Fire for **2 minutes**.

TWO

From position 1, bring the right knee down to the floor, and bend the torso to rest over the thigh. Place the forehead on the floor, stretch the left leg all the way back and rest the arms by your sides, palms up. Relax in the position and breathe slowly and deeply for **3 minutes**.

THREE

Repeat exercise 1 and 2 with the opposite legs.

FOUR Front Bend

Stand up and place your feet about 2 feet apart. Bend over and touch your fingertips or palms to the floor. Hold the pose and do long deep breathing for **3 minutes**. Slowly stand up and relax.

FIVE Ego Eradicator

Standing in the same position, raise your arms overhead at a 30 degree angle, elbows straight. Point the thumbs up and curl the fingers onto the Venus mounds (the fleshy part at the top of the palms just under the fingers). Breathe long and deep for **3 minutes**.

When seated to do Ego Eradicator the arms are at a 60 degree angle; when standing the angle is 30 degrees, as pictured, for balance.

SIX Triangle Pose Come onto your hands and knees and push up into Triangle Pose. The heels remain flat on the floor. Let your head and neck relax and hold the pose for **3 minutes**, then relax on your stomach for **1 minute**.

SEVEN Cobra Pose Lie on your stomach with your heels together and your palms flat on the floor under your shoulders. Push up into Cobra Pose, keeping your hips on the floor ideally. Stretch your head and neck up and begin Long Deep Breathing for **1 minute**. Then for **2 minutes**, slowly turn your head from side to side, inhaling to the left, exhaling to the right. To finish, inhale, exhale and pull Mulbandh a few seconds, then inhale and repeat this sequence 2 more times.

EIGHT

Sit on your heels in Rock Pose with your knees far apart. Bend forward bringing your forehead to the floor, with the palms flat on the floor in front of your knees. Inhale and rise up on the knees, stretching your arms up and out overhead like a flower greeting the sun. Exhale as you come down, and place your forehead on the floor. Continue this motion for **3 minutes**, then inhale and sit up to relax in Rock Pose.

NINE Yoga Mudra

Still in Rock Pose, bring your knees together and interlace your fingers at the base of your spine. Bring your forehead to the floor and lift your arms up straight behind you as high as possible. Hold the position for **3 minutes** with long deep breaths.

Breath Rhythm to Regulate the Pituitary & Pineal Glands

*(originally called **Breath Rhythm to Regulate the Menstrual Cycle**)*

This meditation regulates the rhythm of the breath to stimulate and alternate the pituitary energy, and the pineal radiation which controls the pituitary. This is recommended for men along with the *Pituitary Gland Series*, and the *Kriya for the Aura, Liver & Self-Reliance* on page 43, which cleanses the liver and balances sexual energy.

ONE
Sit in Easy Pose, with your elbows straight, hands resting on the knees, palms facing up. The eyes remain closed, and the spine and neck should be kept straight.

TWO
Inhale through the nose in four parts. As you chant firmly press the tips of the fingers of each hand in turn to your thumb tips. Press the index fingers to the thumbs on the first sniff, the middle fingers to the thumbs on the second sniff, the ring fingers to the thumbs on the third sniff, and the little fingers to the thumbs on the fourth sniff. The exhalation is made in one long stroke.

THREE
Meditate silently on the sounds *Saa Taa Naa Maa* in rhythm with the breath and finger movements.

Saa

Taa

Naa

Maa

Timing: Begin with **3 minutes** and increase 1 minute a day until you reach 7 minutes. Practice for **7 minutes** a day for one week, then add 1 minute a day until you reach **31 minutes**.

Benefits: The rhythm of this four-part breath stimulates the pituitary and pineal, bringing the glands into the proper rhythm. This is especially recommended for men to keep their biorhythm and potency at optimal levels. The aura is strengthened to give a clear and radiant projection, and negative thought patterns can be erased. For women, the newly established balance can help regulate the menstrual cycle.

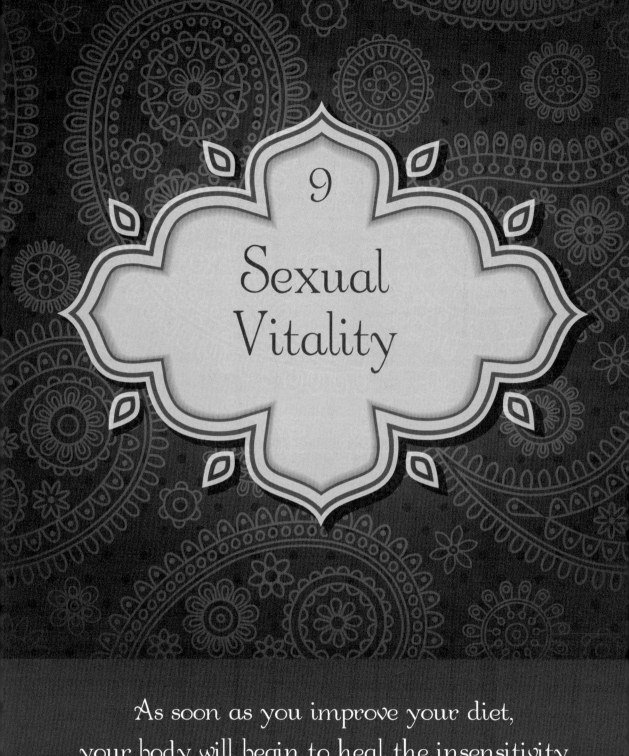

9

Sexual Vitality

As soon as you improve your diet,
your body will begin to heal the insensitivity
of sexual impotency.

What you eat and how you eat has a dramatic impact on your health, sexual vitality, and aging process. Foods that sustain your energy and metabolism help rejuvenate your body, especially if you make it a habit to eat simply, and fill your stomach only halfway.

Temporary Impotency in Men & Women

Overeating by filling your stomach will tax your digestion and can cause temporary impotency in men and women – even at a young age. The best solution for this is to go on liquids, such as the Cardamom-Almond breakfast drink, vegetable soups, and fresh juices. Follow this with a light healthy diet.

Cardamom-Almond Breakfast Drink to Overcome Impotency

> 1 cup water
> 3 cups milk (dairy or non-dairy)
> 20 crushed cardamom pods (use seeds and pods)
> 1 cup almonds (soak and peel skin off)
> 4 Tbsp honey

Boil water, turn off and steep cardamom pods and seeds for 10 minutes. Strain. Blend milk, almonds and cardamom water. Reheat slightly so honey can dissolve in it.

Do not eat solid food for four hours after drinking.

Yogi Bhajan gave the ingredients and specifics about not eating afterwards for four hours; author supplied recipe.

Dietary Recommendations for Women

To enjoy optimal vitality and prevent menstrual problems, women should only eat food which leaves the stomach in two hours and is eliminated in 18 hours, and avoid heavy food especially at night.

Two meals and two nutritious drinks a day are an ideal dietary regimen for women:

- Drink a smoothie or milk with rice bran syrup* for breakfast
- Eat your largest meal at lunch
- Enjoy another nutritious afternoon drink
- Prepare an easily digestible dinner – soup, salad or steamed vegetables

For a woman, eating right is especially important because her constitution is more delicate. Fasting can disturb a woman's navel pulse, adversely affecting her pituitary gland, breasts, and digestion.

Raw leafy greens can cause painful bloating in women, so it is important to soak salads in dressing for at least 15 minutes before eating. An excellent salad dressing for women can be made with lemon juice and olive oil in the summer; substitute sesame oil in the winter.

*After age 18, an ounce of rice bran syrup a day is recommended for women to maintain the proper calcium/magnesium balance.

Foods which cause health issues and decrease a woman's radiance and beauty include salt, sugar, alcohol, coffee, soda and meat, as well as foods that increase acid and cholesterol in the body. Lemons are an excellent substitute for salt in a woman's diet.

Citrus fruit, plums, peaches, papayas, dates, seeds, and raw, cold-pressed unsaturated vegetable oils sustain a woman, as well as foods which facilitate elimination, including green chilies, watermelon, beets, beet greens, and all green vegetables. Eggplant and sesame oil are very energizing for women. Turmeric keeps a woman beautiful, purifies the blood, and heals the internal organs.

Menopausal woman can compensate for the loss of estrogen with vitamin E, chlorophyll, vegetable oils, and almond oil – a mainstay for women. An ounce of raw, cold-pressed almond oil a day should be part of woman's diet after age 28. It helps lower cholesterol, reduce fat, and cleanse toxins from the body. Almond oil is a good source of protein, keeps your skin supple, and alleviates hunger. A great way to incorporate the oil is in a cup of Golden Milk.

Golden Milk

Golden Milk is a delicious, healing bedtime drink. Turmeric, a potent healing root, gives Golden Milk its color and purifies the blood, giving your skin a glow as it heals the internal organs and balances blood sugar. It is essential for the smooth functioning of a woman's reproductive system. The oil and turmeric lubricate the joints, making it excellent for relieving arthritis.

INGREDIENTS:

> 1/8 tsp turmeric
> 1/4 cup water
> 8 oz milk (dairy or non-dairy)
> 2 Tbsp almond oil
> honey or maple syrup

INSTRUCTIONS:

Boil the turmeric in a sauce pan, stirring to a paste for 8 minutes to cook it thoroughly. Heat the milk in a separate sauce pan until it just comes to a boil, remove from the stove. Add the turmeric paste and almond oil to the milk and stir until completely golden. Add honey or maple syrup to taste and drink while warm.

Dietary Recommendations for Men

When your blood chemistry is not correct, the glands cannot support your inner organs. Impotency, disease, and depression are the result. As soon as you improve your diet, your body will begin to heal the insensitivity of sexual impotency.

Your sexual desire will decline when your liver is in trouble. An overtaxed liver impairs the immune system and your ability to heal yourself. Long-term, this stress impairs your sexual performance. One of the best tonics for the liver is beet soup – borscht. Beets are a must for men. Beets purify the bloodstream and beet greens heal the digestive system. Sweet potatoes and water chestnut also rebuild potency.

Beet Soup Recipe

6 medium beets, peeled and chopped. For a sweeter taste, wrap the unpeeled whole beets in foil and roast in the oven at 350°F. After 50-60 minutes, pierce with a fork to see if they are tender. Cool and peel the beets, then chop.

INGREDIENTS:

1 chopped onion
1 chopped leek (white & pale green parts only, rinse well)
2 stalks celery chopped (optional)
3 minced cloves garlic
4 Tbsp olive oil
2 cups vegetable broth
salt & fresh ground pepper
1/8 tsp ginger (optional)
1 sprig fresh parsley (optional)
crème fraîche

INSTRUCTIONS:

Saute the onion, leek, celery, and garlic in olive oil over medium heat for about 10 minutes. Stir often to prevent browning. Cook until soft.
Add the seasonings and beets and cook a few minutes longer, stirring frequently to prevent sticking.
Add the vegetable broth, cover, and simmer 25-30 minutes until the vegetables are tender.
After the soup cools, blend in a food processor in batches.
Lightly reheat and serve with a dollop of crème fraîche.

Healthy Semen Production

It takes 80 drops of digested food to produce one drop of blood, and 80 drops of blood to make one drop of semen. In other words a man's body consumes 640 drops of purely digested food to make one drop of semen. Semen is like oil in a car and food is like gas; if both are of high quality, a man will enjoy good health and sexuality.

Two cloves of garlic a day (taken in food or capsules) will maintain a male's sexual energy and increase semen production. Onions and ghee (clarified butter) are also good for semen production. Ghee should be the main oil a man consumes to prevent sexual problems and keep his weight balanced. Unsalted raw pistachios are also excellent for men.

Cardamom very, very sexual,
Cinnamon, sexual,
Black pepper sexual,
Tomatoes sexual....
Water chestnuts sexual,
Lichi sexual.
Mango super sexual....
Fenugreek sexual,
Eggplant sexual (that's why you like eggplant parmesan.)
Figs with saffron injected, pure, pure, sexual,
Eggs non-sexual.
Meat non-sexual.

–YOGI BHAJAN

Pistachio Parathas

These Pistachio Parathas will strengthen male potency and are helpful for arthritis. One day a week, live on two of these delicious parathas. They are a very pure food – you don't need to eat anything else with them.

DOUGH: ½ cup corn flour (not corn meal)
    ½ cup garbanzo flour
    ½ cup bhajara flour (found in Indian stores, if unavailable
        use whole wheat flour)
    3 cups whole wheat flour

STUFFING: 1 lb. shelled unsalted pistachio nuts
    1 cup minced cauliflower
    1 chopped onion
    2 tsp saffron (soaked overnight in ¼ cup milk)
    1 tsp red chilies
    2 tsp salt
    1 tsp pepper
    ghee (clarified butter)

Blend the stuffing ingredients until they become a fine mixture.

Mix the flours with water to make a dough consistency. After kneading the dough a while, put a golf size ball of the dough on a floured surface. Roll it flat with a rolling pin until it is 6" in diameter. Put ½ cup stuffing in the middle, fold up the sides of the circle and pinch them together to seal the stuffing inside. Roll this out and again flatten into a 6" circle. If any of the stuffing leaks through the dough, patch it with flour.

Place the stuffed paratha in a dry chapati pan or frying pan over a low-medium flame. Cook on one side for 10-15 minutes, then turn it over and pour a little ghee (clarified butter) on top. Cook for 5 minutes longer, pressing down on the paratha with a spoon.

Kriya for the Inner Organs, Glands & Metabolism

Make this set a part of your life for **11 minutes** every day so you'll never have problems with your inner organs or your glands. Do the best you can for as long as you can, working your way up to **3 minutes** for each exercise.

Yogi Bhajan's Comments: "You know you need this set when your weight has increased for no apparent reason, you have acquired fat in the area underneath your navel, your liver is not working well, and your metabolism is not functioning well. This entire set will make your mind fresh – you'll have grit. It takes away fear. You'll experience yourself, you'll feel yourself. Mind will heal itself, body will heal itself."

ONE

Come into Baby Pose by sitting on the heels, bending forward, and bringing your forehead to the floor. Your arms rest at your sides with the palms up. With your shoulders as close to the floor as possible, lift your head and neck, and do Breath of Fire. Start with **2 minutes** and build up to **3 minutes**.

TWO

From Baby Pose, lean back until you are lying on your back with your heels *underneath* your buttocks, arms at your sides. Do Breath of Fire. Start with **1½ minutes** and build up to **3 minutes**.

THREE

Stand up and then squat down keeping your feet flat. Bend forward keeping your back parallel to the floor as best you can. Grasp the outside of your feet by reaching inside and around between your knees. Do Breath of Fire *through your mouth*. Start with **1½ minutes** and build up to **3 minutes**.

FOUR

Sit in Easy Pose with your arms folded at shoulder height parallel to the floor, palms down, right arm resting on the left. Close your eyes and focus at the Third Eye. Breathe very, very slowly – about **12 seconds** per inhalation and **12 seconds** per exhalation. Silently chant: *Haree* 84 times on each inhalation and *Har* 84 times on each exhalation. *Haree* calls upon the Creative energy and *Har* joins the God within and without. **5 minutes**.

Comments: You can extend this set into a full-length class by doing the first three postures for **3 minutes** followed by a **5 minute** relaxation, and repeating this sequence three times.* After the third repetition do the fourth posture for the relaxation. Including the **2 minutes** it takes to transition between postures, it takes **11 minutes** for each repetition of the exercises.

* Editor's Note: these exercises are strenuous; use caution before practicing or teaching three repetitions of 3 minutes each.

Sat Kriya for Better Sex Under Stress

This variation of *Sat Kriya* will keep the Kundalini energy flowing so you can have good sex even when you are under a lot of stress. It releases blocks in the spiral motion of the Kundalini so it can move rhythmically up and down the chakras.

Sit in a tub with warm (not hot) water up to your navel. Practice *Sat Kriya* for **15 minutes** and then lie down and relax in the water. When you are through you will be able to relax and enjoy having sex.

Sat Kriya is an integral part of many Kundalini Yoga sets. As a kriya, it is complete in itself, and can be done with your partner (see page 117) or on your own – follow the instructions that start on page 118.

Yogi Tea

And last but not least, Yogi Tea. A woman should avoid stimulating drinks and substitute Yogi Tea, which is delicious hot or cold. Known for its many health benefits, it is also, according to yogic scriptures on sex, beneficial for women to drink a sweet cup of Yogi Tea before making love. Interestingly, men are advised to drink theirs afterward. For those of who you have only tasted Yogi Tea brewed from a tea-bag, try making it yourself, you are sure to appreciate the difference

~ Sat Nam ~

Start with ten ounces of water per cup and brew at least four cups at once. For each cup, add:

> 3 cloves
> 4 green crushed cardamom pods (crushed)
> 4 peppercorns
> ½ stick cinnamon
> 1 slice ginger root

Boil 20-30 minutes. Then add ¼ teaspoon black tea.
After 2 minutes, add ½ cup milk per cup of liquid.
Heat just to the boiling point, remove, and strain immediately.
Add honey to taste.

10

Kundalini Yoga Basics

Consciousness is biological in nature.
It is controlled by the secretion of
chemicals in the brain.

The Yoga of Awareness

Kundalini Yoga is designed to give an experience of elevation and well-being by raising the flow of energy, known as the Kundalini. Consciousness is biological in nature; it is controlled by the secretion of chemicals in the brain. When the Kundalini rises it activates these chemicals, creating significant changes in consciousness. With consistent practice of Kundalini Yoga, your heart opens and changes occur on every level of your life – body, mind, and soul.

Create a Comfortable Environment

Use a cushioned mat, natural fiber blanket or a sheepskin ideally (to protect you from the earth's electromagnetic field). Select a quiet place where you will not be interrupted. It is best to do yoga on an empty stomach. When you practice yoga many emotions can arise in the process of transformation. Drinking water will balance you emotionally.

Wear comfortable clothing made of natural fibers. Wearing white is recommended as it is psychologically uplifting and expands your aura. It's a good idea to use a shawl during meditation to keep your spine warm. A head covering will strengthen your electromagnetic field and contain the energy that circulates to your brain. Keep your feet bare to conduct electromagnetic energy through the body's nervous system.

Warm-Ups

The Kundalini Yoga kriyas in this book contain some advanced postures. It is important to spend time warming up before beginning these kriyas to increase your flexibility and avoid injury. Recommended warm-ups include: Spinal Flex, Cat-Cow, Life Nerve Stretch, pranayam, and any short Kundalini Yoga kriya, such as *Healing Hands* on page 84. If you are a beginner, start with the minimum time given for each posture and keep a steady rhythm as you increase your pace.

Yoga During Menstruation & Pregnancy

During the heavy days of your menstrual cycle, avoid strenuous yoga postures such as Stretch Pose, Breath of Fire, Bow Pose, Camel Pose, Locust Pose, Leg Lifts, Mulbandh, Sat Kriya, Shoulder Stand, or any of the inverted postures.

After the 120th day of pregnancy, or earlier if there are medical complications, a woman should *not* practice strenuous exercises. Also, a woman should not do yoga or meditation where the breath is held out during pregnancy, as this could deprive the fetus of oxygen. Meditations that involve holding the breath in are fine, as long as the breath is held in no longer than 20 seconds. This strengthens the diaphragm and helps a woman prepare for birth.

Yogic Breathing – Pranayam

Pranayam is the science of utilizing the breath for optimal vitality and peace of mind. Since the mind follows the rate of the breath, changing your breathing patterns creates profound changes in your internal universe. Unless specified otherwise, breathe in and out through the nose only during Kundalini Yoga and meditation.

Long Deep Breathing

By taking a deep yogic breath you can expand your lung capacity nearly eight-fold. As you inhale, your navel and abdomen move outward, then you fill the chest, upper ribs and clavicle. On the exhale release the breath from the top down, and pull your navel and abdomen in to push all the breath out. Be sure to exhale completely to empty the lungs, which will facilitate a deeper inhalation.

Long Deep Breathing develops endurance and patience. If you slow your breath to eight breaths per minute, your pituitary gland secretes fully. If the breath is slowed to four breaths per minute the pineal gland is stimulated, and deep meditation is automatic.

Breath of Fire

In Breath of Fire your breath is powerful, continuous and rapid through the nose only, about 2 to 3 breaths per second. Breath of Fire is powered from the navel point and solar plexus. As you exhale the breath is expelled powerfully through the nose by pressing your navel and solar plexus toward the spine. As you inhale the upper abdominal muscles relax, and the diaphragm extends down. The breath seems to come in as part of relaxation rather than through effort. There is no pause between the inhale and exhale and equal power is given to both.

Breath of Fire releases toxins and expands your lung capacity, strengthens the navel, increases vitality, and repairs the balance between the sympathetic and parasympathetic nervous systems to increase your resistance to stress.

Eye Focus: the Third Eye or Brow Point

Unless otherwise instructed, your eyes remain closed and focused between the eyebrows and up about ¼" at the Third Eye or Brow Point. This stimulates the pituitary gland and allows you to focus on the movements, breath, and mantra involved.

Meditation

When you meditate your brain needs more blood circulation than the body. By sitting with crossed legs in Easy Pose, you slow the circulation to the lower half of the body and more blood supply is available for the brain. The spine is kept straight so the serum can move up and you reach a meditative state much faster than otherwise. In this way, yogis can expand their creative intelligence through meditation.

Mantras

Mantras are often linked with the breath to enhance their ability to direct the mind through rhythmic repetition. Unless otherwise instructed, mentally repeat *Sat* as you inhale and *Nam* as you exhale while doing Kundalini Yoga. *Sat* is pronounced **Sut** (rhymes with but), and *Nam* is pronounced **Naam** (rhymes with mom). *Sat Nam* means Truth is my identity.

Another common mantra, *Wahe Guru*, describes the bliss of going from the darkness of ignorance to the experience of the light within. It is pronounced *wha-hay guroo*.

Mudras

Kundalini Yoga contains many mudras – specific hand and finger positions – which enable you to guide reflexes to the brain. Each mudra gives a clear message to the mind and body energy system. For example, Gyan Mudra stimulates wisdom and increases receptivity and calmness.

Bandhas or Body Locks

The bandhas are locks which direct the flow of life energy within the body and the aura. They consolidate the effects of your efforts, enabling you to bring about subtle transformation.

Mulbandh or Root Lock

Mulbandh is a smooth rapid motion that consists of three parts: contracting the muscles of the sphincter inward and upward; contracting the area around the sex organ as if trying to stop the flow of urine; and contracting the lower abdominal muscles and navel point toward the spine.

Mulbandh stimulates the flow of spinal fluid. Unless otherwise stated, apply Mulbandh at the end of every yoga posture. It can be applied with the breath held in or out. Use only the muscles necessary to hold the lock.

Jalandhar Bandh
aka Neck or Chin Lock

This lock is generally applied when holding the breath in or out, with Mulbandh, and during chanting meditations. To apply Neck Lock pull the spine straight, lift the chest up, and at the same time gently stretch the back of the neck by pulling the chin in to allow the flow of energy through the neck. Do not bring the head down; bring the chest up to increase mobility in your upper back. Keep your face and neck muscles relaxed.

Jalandhar Bandh opens the energy of the *medulla oblongata* in the brain stem, and allows the energy to flow more effectively to the pineal and pituitary glands in the brain. When the pituitary rotates, the "cup of nectar" (the secretion of the pituitary) flows down to the heart and your Kundalini is awakened.

Sitting Postures

Easy Pose and Rock Pose are the two commonly used sitting postures in Kundalini Yoga *kriyas* (yoga sets) and meditations. Easy Pose is done sitting in a comfortable cross-legged position, and Rock Pose is done sitting on your heels. In both postures, sit with your spine straight, and your chin tucked in slightly.

Kundalini Yoga Music

Music is instrumental in enhancing the effects of pranayam, mantra, and meditation in Kundalini Yoga. Yogi Bhajan specified that we play only 3HO music in Kundalini Yoga classes – its subtle rhythms create inner energy and elevation.

Relaxation

To get the maximum benefit from the kriyas, it is important to rest between postures unless otherwise instructed. If you are a beginner, and especially if the kriya is strenuous, relax in Easy Pose or Corpse Pose for 30 seconds to 3 minutes between exercises. This allows the energy generated, and the glandular secretions released, to circulate throughout your body.

Corpse Pose is done lying on your back with your hands by your sides, palms facing up, ankles uncrossed, and your feet relaxed. Cover yourself to contain the energy you've created and stay warm. After completing a kriya, it is important to relax for 5 to 10 minutes in Corpse Pose. Afterwards, roll your ankles and wrists a few times in each direction, hug your knees, and rock on your spine a few times, and then sit up. At this time you may choose to continue with a meditation, or end your yoga session with the *Long Time Sun* song.

Closing Song

Kundalini yogis traditionally sing the following song to end a yoga class:

May the long time sun shine upon you,

All love surround you, and the pure light within you,

Guide your way on.

May the long time sun shine upon you,

All love surround you, and the pure light within you,

Guide your way on, guide your way on, guide your way on.

Inhale deeply to chant: *Saaaaaaaaaaaaat Nam*. You may choose to end with a silent prayer or by bringing your forehead to the floor briefly.

Sat Nam

Yogi Bhajan,
Master of Kundalini Yoga
(1929-2004)

Yogi Bhajan, Ph.D., Master of Kundalini Yoga and Mahan Tantric of White Tantric Yoga, came to the West in 1969. Recognizing the deep desire of young people to experience higher consciousness, he taught Kundalini Yoga, and founded 3HO Foundation – the Healthy, Happy, Holy Organization.

Yogi Bhajan inspired and counseled people for over 34 years with his unique wisdom, humor, and compassion. He gave over 8,000 recorded lectures, and authored many books to carry his teachings forward into the Aquarian Age. Thanks to his vision, White Tantric Yoga and Kundalini Yoga Teacher Training programs are widely available internationally, and 3HO Summer and Winter Solstices and Yoga Festivals continue to grow.

Yogi Bhajan, known affectionately as Yogiji to hundreds of thousands worldwide, always said that his mission was "to create teachers, not collect students." Thousands of Kundalini Yoga teachers follow in his footsteps today, making it their mission to share *Kundalini Yoga as Taught by Yogi Bhajan*™.

About the Authors

Nam Kaur began studying with Yogi Bhajan in 1973 and has been teaching Kundalini Yoga for over 35 years. She founded the 3HO International Kundalini Yoga Teachers Association (IKYTA) in 1994. As CEO of the Kundalini Research Institute (KRI), she coordinated the creation of the KRI International Teacher Training Certification program, and worked closely with Yogi Bhajan on the Aquarian Teacher Textbook.

Nam Kaur and her husband travel internationally to offer workshops such as: *The Healing Essence of Kundalini Yoga*, *Sun Energy for the Lunar Woman*, *Creating a Spiritual Biosphere*, and *The Stages of Spiritual Growth*. The authors also offer personal Yogic Consultations while on tour and year-round by telephone and Skype.

Siri Atma Singh Khalsa, M.D., is an engaging speaker in the field of yoga, healing and medicine. An Internist and Hospitalist, Dr. Siri Atma Singh also holds an undergraduate degree in Philosophy & Religion. He was trained by Yogi Bhajan and served as his personal physician for eight years. Yogi Bhajan called him a medical intuitive and a pure healer, which aptly describe his ability to tune into what people need at a very deep level in order to heal. Dr. Siri Atma Singh is the author of a Kundalini Yoga book on the Ten Bodies entitled, *Waves of Healing: Listening to the Voice of Your Soul*.

Resources

Nam Kaur & Siri Atma Singh Khalsa, M.D.

To view the authors Teaching Schedule, arrange for a Yogic Consultation, order their book on the Ten Bodies, *Waves of Healing: Listening to the Voice of Your Soul*, or DVD workshop lectures, please visit: www.DrSiriAtma.com.

Recommended Reading

Yogi Bhajan, *The Teachings of Yogi Bhajan: The Power of the Spoken Word*

Yogi Bhajan, *The Aquarian Teacher: KRI Level 1 Textbook & Yoga Manual*

Shakti Parwha Kaur Khalsa, *Kundalini Yoga: The Flow of Eternal Power*

Mukta Kaur Khalsa: *Meditations for Addictive Behavior*

Akal Sahai Singh (Steve Coffing): *Be the Lighthouse, Divine Love*, & more

Arnbjörg Kristín Konráðsdóttir: *True Nature - Iceland: Kundalini Yoga Meditations in Icelandic Nature*

Yogi Bhajan Every Day Quotes: Desk calendars, www.aquarianwisdom.com

3HO

For a Kundalini Yoga teacher: www.ikyta.org/search/teachers

For White Tantric Yoga schedule: www.whitetantricyoga.com

For Kundalini Yoga books and music:

Ancient Healing Ways:	www.a-healing.com
Spirit Voyage:	www.spiritvoyage.com
Yoga Technology:	www.yogatech.com
Sat Nam Versand (Europe):	www.satnam.eu
Nam Publishers (Spanish):	www.nampublishers.com
Be the Lighthouse:	www.bethelighthouse.com

References

Special Thanks To......

Aquarian Wisdom Daily Inspiration Calendar (AW) quotes, compiled by Darshan Kaur Khalsa and Satya Kaur Khalsa

Aquarian Times Magazine (AT) for the majority of the yoga sets in *Divine Relationships*

KRI for **I Am A Woman (IAAW) quotes; Man to Man**: The Men's Teachings of Yogi Bhajan, KRI 2009; The Aquarian Teacher™ KRI International Kundalini Yoga Teacher Training Level I Textbook & Yoga Manual (**AT Textbook/AT Yoga Manual**); Yogi Bhajan Lectures (**YB Lecture**)

1 Two Bodies, One Soul - wlAAW, 7-26-82; 1989 Beads of Truth 3rd quarter / The Ten Bodies - YB Lecture, 8-22-78; 12-30/31-85; AW, 6-18-11/6-17-92; **Waves of Healing: Listening to the Voice of Your Soul (Waves of Healing)**, Yogic Reality Inc., 2009, Siri Atma Singh Khalsa, M.D., pg. 50-59

2 Attracting a Spiritual Partner - YB Lecture, 5-10-85; 12-30/31-85 / Flirtation - AT Summer 2002; YB Lecture, 7-6-02; 7-31-84; 7-5-93; 7-12-84; IAAW, 7-23-84; **Shatki the Sacred Essence & Power of Women (Shakti the Sacred Essence)**, 3HO Women, Editor: Sat Kirpal Kaur Khalsa, Ph.D., 2005, pg. 62 / Kriya to Release the Pain of the Past & Energize Your Current Relationship - AT Summer 2003 / Kirtan Kriya - Waves of Healing, pgs. 193-196; AT Yoga Manual, pg. 426 / Grace of God Meditation - Waves of Healing, pgs. 190-192

3 The Difference Between the Sexes. YB Lecture, 6-30-93; 7-6-00; 7-1-94; **Marriage on the Spiritual Path,** KRI 2007, Shakti Parwha Kaur Khalsa, pg. 37; YB Lecture, 6-30-93; 7-6-00; 7-1-94; Shakti the Sacred Essence, pg. 74; Man to Man, 9-3-78 / Lovemaking - YB Lecture, **There's Nothing in Sex and Without Sex There is Nothing (Nothing in Sex)**; 10-11-87; 8-24-76; Man to Man, pg. 15; **Understanding Sexual Behavior**, Beads of Truth, Spring 1977 / Mending a Man's Heart - YB Lecture, 8-14-97; Beads of Truth, Spring 1977; Shakti the Sacred Essence, pg. 86 / The Power of Woman - YB Lecture, 7-94, **Five Lectures, Five Decades: The Power of Woman** / A Woman's Purity - AT Summer 2002, pg. 32; YB Lecture, 8-14-97; 8-24-76; Shakti the Sacred Essence, pg. 83; AT Yoga Manual, pg. 328 / Fear of Men - AT Summer 2002, pg. 66 / The Art of Long Deep Breathing - Kundalini Yoga for Youth & Joy, pg 7; AT Summer 2001, pg. 65 / Sodarshan Chakra Kriya - AT Yoga Manual, pg. 420 / Kriya for the Aura, Positivity & Vitality - AT Summer 2003, pg. 41

4 The Nature of the Sexes. YB Lecture, 7-8-96 / Containing a Man - YB Lecture, 7-5-93; 6-30-93; 6-25-92; Beads of Truth, Spring 77 / Reflecting a Man - YB Lecture, 7-12-89; 7-29-81; 6-30-93; 6-25-92; 8-4-83; 7-12-84; 12-7-97; 6-25-01; **Relax & Rejoice: A Marriage Manual by Yogi Bhajan, (Relax & Rejoice)** Vol. 1, 1982; Beads of Truth, Winter 1983 / Creative Communication - YB Lecture, 7-5-93; 7-3-80; 6-30-97; 1-23-90; 7-12-89; 8-4-80; 8-24-76; IAAW, 6-28-88; AW, 7-20-84 / Pillow Talk - YB Lecture, 6-30-97 / Kriya for the Aura, Liver & Self-Reliance - AT Spring 2003, pgs. 36-37 / Narayan Kriya to Knit the Tears in Your Relationship - AT May-June 2009, pg. 18

5 Married in Love. Beads of Truth, 3rd quarter 1989; Beads of Truth, Spring 1977; YB Lecture, 10- 11-87; 3-20-87; IAAW, 7-15-84; Ending Quote: YB Lecture, 10-11-87 / Merging Two Souls - YB Lecture, 5-30-85; 10-17-79; 5-7-91; 3-20-87; AW, 10-7-99/5-12-12; **Man Called the Siri Singh Sahib**, Sikh Dharma, 1979, pg. 168; www.WhiteTantricYoga.com / Creating Intimacy - AW, 7-13-94/11-10-12; Beads of Truth, Spring 1977 / Recharge Yourself - AT Summer 2003, pg. 41 / Long Ek Ong Kars for Couples - 3HO E-newsletter, 2-16-12 / Meditation for Marital & Financial Stability - Relax and Rejoice, Vol. 2

6 Living in Harmony. Waves of Healing, pg. 173; AW, 7-28-81/6-10-10; Beads of Truth, Spring 1977; YB Lecture, 7-5-93 / How to Stay Married in Love - YB Lecture, 8-14-97; 6-30-97; AW, 3-2-12/ 8-11-99; Beads of Truth, Winter 1982; Man to Man, 9-3-78; AT Summer 2001, pg. 67; IAAW, 11-17-12/6-27-88 / Humor - Shakti the Sacred Essence, pg. 63; YB Lecture, 8-4-83 / Sweet Talk - YB Lecture, 12-7-97; 7-3-80; IAAW, 7-12-84; Ending quote: IAAW, 2-22-13/7-1-87 / Meditation for Speaking Consciously - **Harmonious Communication by Yogi Bhajan**, Vikram Kaur Khalsa & Dharm Darshan Kaur Khalsa, 1987, pg. 47 / Foot Massage - AW, 1-13-11/5-1-85 / Communication by the Stars - Harmonious Communication, pgs. 30-33 / Healing Hands - AT Spring 2004, pg. 20 / Relaxation Series to Remove Negativity & Tension - AT Summer 2001 pgs. 38-39 / Kirtan Kriya for Couples to Clear the Clouds - Relax & Rejoice, Vol.1, pg. 91

7 Sex -The Sixth Sense. YB Lecture, 10-11-87; Nothing in Sex / The Trigger for Sex - YB Lecture, 6-25-92; 8-14-97; 7-8-96; Shakti the Sacred Essence, pg. 61; The Washington Post, 11-18-86; Shakti the Sacred Essence, pg. 62, 88 /

Sex for Breakfast, Lunch & Dinner - YB Lecture, 9-13-69; 12-74 Winter Solstice; Nothing in Sex; 5-9-96; Shakti the Sacred Essence, pgs. 78-79; Man to Man, 9-3-78 / Foreplay - YB Lecture, 8-14-97 / Orgasm - Beads of Truth, Spring 77; Shakti the Sacred Essence, pg. 77; Relax & Rejoice, Vol. 2; YB Lecture, 6-25-92; 8-14-97 / Interlock Intercourse - YB Lecture, 6-25-92 / Strengthening the Kegels - www.mayoclinic.com/health/kegel-exercises / Pelvic Pleasure - Shakti the Sacred Essence, pg. 86 / Formula for Ecstasy - YB Lecture, 6-25-92; Shakti the Sacred Essence, pgs. 83, 88 / Prolonging Erection - YB Lecture, 8-14-97 / Post-Sex Rejuvenation - YB Lecture, 5-30-85; 7-13-94; 7-3-89; Man to Man, pg. 59; **The Art of Making Sex Sacred**, Jiwan Joti Kaur Khalsa, Ph.D., 2nd Edition, 2009, pg 141 / Male Maintenance - Man to Man, pg. 344 / Youth & Vitality for Women - Shakti the Sacred Essence, pgs. 78-79; YB Lecture, 6-25-92; The Art of Making Sex Sacred, pg.141 / Post-Sex Stretches for Women - YB Lecture, 6-25-92; AT Yoga Manual pg. 361, 372; **A Woman's Book of Yoga: Embracing Our Natural Life Cycles**, Avery Trade 2002, by Machelle M. Seibel, MD and Hari Kaur Khalsa / Kriya for Nervous System & Glandular Balance - AT Spring 2001 /Sat Kriya for Couples - AT Summer 2002, pg. 67; AT Yoga Manual, pg. 348

8 Sexual Potency. YB Lecture, 8/14/97; 6-25-97; 8-4-97; Beads of Truth, Winter 82 / Sexual Pituitary Control - Wikipedia; Man to Man, Fall 1981 pg. 30 / Premature Ejaculation - Shakti the Sacred Essence, pg. 83 / Male Maturation - Man to Man, Fall 1981; Shakti the Sacred Essence, pg. 61; YB Lecture, 6-25-92 / Best Times to Have (and Not Have) Sex - AT Summer 2002, pg. 66; Beads of Truth, Spring 1977; YB Lecture, 8-16/18-85; 7-13-94; Man to Man, 8-14-97 / Pituitary Gland Series - AT Yoga Manual, pg. 373 / *Breath Rhythm to Regulate the Pituitary & Pineal Glands* - Lunar Woman: IKYTA, Hari Charn Kaur Khalsa, 1995, pg. 29

9 Sexual Vitality. Beads of Truth, Winter 1982, No. 10; YB Lecture, 6-25-92; 8-14-97; Golden Milk recipe - **Kundalini Yoga: The Flow of Eternal Power,** Perigee Trade 1998, Shakti Parwha Kaur Khalsa; Pistachio Parathas recipe - www.3ho.org / Kriya for the Inner Organs, Glands & Metabolism - Beads of Truth, 11-21-84 / Sat Kriya for Better Sex under Stress - AT Summer 2002, pg. 66

10 Kundalini Yoga Basics. Waves of Healing, pgs. 100-107; Meditation - YB Lecture, 10-17-79; Mantra - AT Textbook, pg. 87

Index